♥ ♥ ♥

A Voice From Heaven

♥ ♥ ♥

By Sheree Silver

Copyright © 2004 by Sheree Silver

All rights reserved. No part of this book shall be reproduced or transmitted in any form or by any means, electronic, mechanical, magnetic, photographic including photocopying, recording or by any information storage and retrieval system, without prior written permission of the publisher. No patent liability is assumed with respect to the use of the information contained herein. Although every precaution has been taken in the preparation of this book, the publisher and author assume no responsibility for errors or omissions. Neither is any liability assumed for damages resulting from the use of the information contained herein.

ISBN 0-7414-1851-7

Cover design by Thomas Addison of
Addison Fitzgerald Studios, Inc.
St. Augustine, Florida
www.addfitz.com

Author's photo by Betsy Lee.
www.betsyleephotography.com

Published by:

519 West Lancaster Avenue
Haverford, PA 19041-1413
Info@buybooksontheweb.com
www.buybooksontheweb.com
Toll-free (877) BUY BOOK
Local Phone (610) 520-2500
Fax (610) 519-0261

Printed in the United States of America

Printed on Recycled Paper

Published February 2004

I dedicate this book to my boys, Andrew and Justin. Know that you are never alone . . .

Acknowledgments

- Thanks to God, my guides and helpers, for all your guidance and protection in my life.

- A special warm hug to Poppa for your knowledge, help and encouragement in completing this book.

- Gratitude to my birth family for your support and wisdom through the years.

- To my friends who helped make this book possible, especially Carol and Barbara. I couldn't have done it without you.

- To my partner Sam, for teaching and showing me unconditional love, and helping to make my dreams come true.

- Many thanks to my clients and students who have taught me so much.

- A very special hug and kiss to my incredible boys–my love for you is unending. Thank you for allowing me to be your mum.

Introduction

I was born Sheree Lynne Jackson on December 8, 1958, in London, England and was the first born child. Two years later my brother, Colin was born and then four years later my sister, Karen arrived. I believe I was born psychic; I seemed to hear everyone's thoughts and could feel their energy, however this was certainly not an advantage in our dysfunctional family.

I remember often feeling very sad and resorted to food for comfort, especially chocolate. When my parents divorced, I was eight years old and life definitely took a turn for the better. My mother and I went to live with my step father whom I really liked. His daughter, Michelle was a friend of mine and we were both close in age. My brother and sister went to live with our father. I would go to visit them on one weekend and they would come to visit us the next.

Michelle eventually went to live with her mother and my sister, Karen came to live with us. My brother, Colin always stayed with our father. Eventually, our mother married our step father and Michelle's mother married my father. Yes, they switched partners. The affairs were going on before the divorce, but as children we were unaware of it.

Weekends at Dad's were rough. Colin would always get a new toy or game, which created a lot of jealousy and arguments that caused resentment in me.

I was a regular teenager; I had crushes on boys and went to dances every weekend. At age 11, I looked like I was 15. I attended a public Jewish school, which was 1 ½ hours from our house. I had to ride two trains and finally a bus to get to school. I would leave at 7:30 a.m. and get back home at the end of the day at 6:00 p.m.

My grandfather, whom I called Poppa, would visit us often and give us pocket money.

The highlight of my childhood was our vacations. We would go to Italy and Spain for two weeks each year and it was what kept me sane.

When I was 12, my mother and stepfather started attending the SAGB, aka Spiritual Association of Great Britain. It was a center for spiritual development. They were training to be psychics. I would often go with them on Sunday. I remember the first time I went, a man was standing up in front of the audience giving them messages from their loved ones on the other side. I sat spellbound watching while some people were crying and others were happy.

I was deeply affected by my first visit to the center. This was the beginning of my spiritual journey; I started reading nonstop. The first book I read was *The World Beyond* by Ruth Montgomery. In her book, she reported that she would sit at her typewriter and receive messages from Arthur Ford, a medium she had interviewed when he was on Earth. She described the other side and provided explanations for so many things. It all felt right to me. Her books brought a deeper sense of peace into my life.

At age 15, we went to live in America–the Bronx New York to be exact. My Poppa had immigrated to America a year earlier. When summer came, we moved to New Jersey and in September of that year, I began attending Elmwood Park High School. I liked this school right away for two reasons: the school was only five minutes from our house, and I was pretty popular because I was from England. I joined the theater department and started to perform in plays and musicals. After I graduated from high school, we moved to California and I studied theater at Cypress College.

My Poppa remained in New York, but would visit us in California every couple of years. At 21, I moved out of the house for the first time. At first, I worked as a waitress, and then after getting my Associates' degree, I became a bank teller. It paid the bills, but it was not very fulfilling work.

I enjoyed reading books on self-improvement and spiritual growth. I learned to meditate and this brought balance to all the personal relationships that I had.

At age 26, I met my husband, Scott Silver, at a Jewish single's dance. We were married the following year which was 1986. Soon after our marriage, I quit my job as an escrow secretary. I was not sure what I would do, but within a couple of months I went to a lecture on hypnosis and found it fascinating. I signed up for the class and became a certified hypnotist. This was a dream come true.

I started my hypnosis business in 1987 and helped people from my home. I loved it and for the first time in my life I felt completely fulfilled.

After a few years I took a trip to visit my dad in England and I went to the Spiritual Association of Great Britain and had a psychic reading. The lady doing my reading picked up on the work I was doing and told me it was time for me to begin doing psychic readings also. I admit this made me a little nervous, but I decided to give it a try. As my confidence grew, my practice expanded to include psychic readings. I often appeared on radio talk shows and gave lectures on hypnosis, past life regression and the psychic field.

In 1993, at age 35, I was ready to be a mum and conceived Andrew Elijah. He was born February 9, 1994. He weighed 9 pounds, 9 ounces. He was a wonderful baby and even though my marriage was not the best, I was happy being a mum.

We left California in 1994 and moved to Colorado where business was very slow for me. I saw my Poppa for the last time just before we left for Colorado. Poppa and I talked a lot that day as we walked around the mall. I asked him about his life with my Nana (his wife who died when I was 3), and I also mentioned that when he died he should write to me from the other side. Part of me was serious, the other part of me was just joking.

When we said goodbye, I felt a closeness to him like I had not felt before. We lived in Colorado for two years and our second son, Justin Ryan, was born on January 5, 1997. We had a terrible snow storm that same year and decided to move to St. Augustine, Florida. It is the oldest city of the United States, and it is where I continue to do my spiritual work which includes hypnosis and psychic readings.

This book covers two years of my life from 1999 to 2001. It is a collection of conversations that I had with my grandfather in Heaven. I discussed many subjects with him. He became my confidant, helping me to have courage and faith that I was loved and well protected.

♥ ♥ ♥

Poppa was born, Samuel Cohen, on December 26, 1909 in Whitechapel, London. He was twelve years old when his parents died and he was sent to an orphanage. He was separated from his brothers until years later after he moved to New York when they reunited. While in the orphanage, he was badly treated and eventually left at age 15.

Poppa worked as a tailor most of his life. During World War II, he remained a civilian, but he was given the designation of 'Air Warden,' with the responsibility of making sure everyone in town was safe.

He met Kitty Finklestein (my Nana) when he attended a political talk in Whitechapel. He instantly fell in love with her. They married and had two children: my mother, Lea and my uncle, Eddie. They shared a wonderful marriage, had lots of friends and enjoyed going out dancing. Poppa fancied sports, especially English football and horse racing.

Kitty died at age 49 in 1961. Poppa never remarried. He moved to America in 1973 to be with his brothers in New York, where he lived a contented, peaceful life until his death in 1996 at age 87.

♥ ♥ ♥

Before my grandfather passed on, we discussed having him contact me from the other side and sharing what it was like. A few years after he died, he came to me in a dream reminding me of this conversation. I thought about it for a while. Since I had done a little channeled writing in the past, I decided this would be a good way for us to communicate with each other.

I held my pen and asked for protection from God. I requested to talk to my grandfather. After about ten minutes, I heard a voice in my head and felt compelled to write. This was what flowed onto the paper.

♥ ♥ ♥

1

October 10, 1999

Hello Poppa,

I am so glad you are here, Sheree. There is no separation. The veil is an illusion. Life and death are the same. Time is not real. We all are the plan. From here or there, we are all in a zone of complete oneness. Time is a worldly perception, a necessity to keep the attention. The way we live on this side is we allow a thought to come and then we follow it to the next idea, which leads to the complete picture. It's not one before the other. It's the same.

When man is at the point of a zone of never-ending life spans, then we will see the breaking away of the time warp. In that space, time will stand still. The weather will be a matter of direction. If we need snow, it will snow. If we need sun, it will be sunny. Whatever we need, the atmosphere will come in line with the size of the planet or ozone layer.

The necessity to grow is a big challenge to us as well. We each have a mission and it's not in line with Earth, it's in conjunction with the soul's development. When we knew each other, I was your grandfather and you were my granddaughter. There was a separation in time but not in spirit. We are the same. No separation exists. In dreams, we can come together. No time separation. No illusion.

Where is Heaven and what is it like?
Heaven is like the wind, Sheree. The wind blows things around from place to place. It has no starting or ending place. Heaven just is. It's not a place like Italy or Spain–it's not a trip you make in a plane. It is a state of being.

It's the same as Earth. We are there and nowhere else. We live the same life as you. We see you. We are in you. We are all life. Each aspect adds to the other.

I am having a hard time understanding.
I know–life is an illusion, it's like a magic show. You think the magician is making something vanish, yet it's still there. It seems like we die or disappear, but we have not gone anywhere.

How can you be here with us? Where do you live?
It's not a matter of living. We are not solid, yet we can be if we want to. We are all thought, all matter, all water, all ocean, all wind. We are consciousness. If we want to sit under a tree, we see a tree. The thought of the tree produces the tree. If we want to rest in a house, the thought of the house produces a place to rest. On this side, it is all creation.

Is there a collective place that is fixed?
No, not in the way you think. For example, if there is an understanding that a class will take place in a building, we all collectively agree to meet in this building. When it's time, we think about the building and the class and in the blink of an eye we are there.

Do you talk like we do on Earth, using your voice and your body?
We are not a body, yet we have a body if we need it. We appear to each other in thought. For example, I spoke to you and I was just thinking your name. All of a sudden the thought popped into your head, "I should write to Poppa." I call you, Sheree, not with a voice, but with a thought. That's how we communicate with each other here. We think of the person we want to talk to, then that person picks up our request and appears in a so-called body. Our request produces an image. Sometimes we don't need their image; we feel their energy.

Now that's what I call networking! Do you become solid like us on Earth?
Solid only takes place in gravity. It's like an astronaut; he is floating. Earth pulls us into solid matter. Birth keeps us grounded. When we leave, we are free of gravity. It's a release–a freedom that's wonderful. It's a separation from heaviness.

Do you have a job, Poppa?
Job, what's a job? My job is to 'Be'. I am many things, yet we are one. There is no separation. I, we, and you are the same.

Do you eat?
It's not necessary. If a dolphin eats a fish, we eat. If a tiger eats a monkey, we eat. If a monkey eats a banana, we eat. We are dolphin, monkey, and banana. We are consciousness.

How do you communicate with me if you are not alive?
We are mind. We are one. You hear me. I hear you when you talk to me. I enter the separation between your thoughts. You hear me in everything. You remember me as a single being; yet I am all beings.

As I talk, it's like you feel me–I am there, yet I am everywhere. I can laugh yet I can cry. I can talk and I can fly. I am all emotion. I am ALL.

How can you be everything?
It's like a huge park. Everything is there; wind, trees, grass, lake, birds, insects, fish, frogs, man, squirrels. All of nature is represented. Then the whole is one. Do not look with your eyes. In the silence everything is one, all part of the whole but appears separate. You know me as separate but I am everywhere.

This sounds like something that describes God. Poppa, you are not God!
That's interesting yet not accurate. When we leave Earth, illusion is lifted. We see the face of God in the mirror and we are looking at ourselves. We learn and realize God is not an entity alone. God is in everything. We are in everything. We are God.

What is the purpose of being separate from each other?
Fun–a game.

If life is fun, a game, why is it so hard?
Our beliefs make it difficult because they keep us stuck in fear.

I'm getting tired. We'll talk again.
Bye.

2

October 11, 1999

Thank you for coming Poppa.
I am always with you Sheree, we are never separate. Your life is very important to me. You and I are one.

That's very hard to understand.
I know, and I will try to explain. What affects you, affects me. It's a chain reaction, one piece into another. It can't work unless each piece fits like a jigsaw puzzle.

You are very important to the whole. The life you have chosen will impact many people. The promise we made together is the result of eons of preparation. The time is now to share your knowledge. You are very wise. Remember, we are all teachers. Students sometimes and other times we are the teachers. You are part of the never-ending cycle–the link. All links in the chain need to be together to work.

It's hard to know where to begin. I feel my days are so busy.
Do you remember what I said yesterday about time? Just let one thing lead to another. Don't be so occupied with results. They will take care of themselves. When you do what you have to, the end result will be the way you want. The way to get there is to let it unfold. No more doubts. The reason the majority of people are stuck is they are trying to control a part that is not their part to control.

Will my children's book get published and do well?
Another question filled with doubt. Doubt is very destructive, an important thing to wipe out. Your book is a creation and as such, has to have a crescendo, if not today, sometime. Nothing is by accident. Things will unfold to allow your dreams to come true.

Are there real miracles?
That is crazy, Sheree. You know there are miracles; just look at us writing to each other.

Yes, but how do I know it's you, Poppa?
That will have to be trusted.

Okay. What do you have to teach me?
This day is here to explore. Each day is a symbol, a creation. When time is no more, the panic of the world will cease. The Karma will end. Joy will reign.

When will this happen?
It's easy to dismiss joy. It's the first thing man brushes aside. The truth is, it can happen now if man wants it. There are always excuses to stay stuck. It's a blessing to make time for yourself. So let go of your restrictions.

Poppa, it's like there is a part of me that is filled with doubt...
I know, Darling. A reprogramming is needed. Make yourself a tape and go to the origin of your doubt and release it. The world teaches you to have a lack of confidence in yourself and others. It's not necessary to live that way.

Wherever you are, do you experience doubt?
Absolutely...but not in the way you do. We feel doubt in reaching people because they are so closed. We need you all to wake up!

Will the world wake up?
We hope so.

Why don't you know? Isn't everything known in Heaven?
No, life is unraveling as we speak. Each moment is a creation. We don't know if we will reach you. We try, but eons pass when we can't.

Are Uncle Eddie and Nana with you?
They and I and you are one. Yet they are still separate. We experience ourselves apart when we need to and yet we are still one.

What else do you have to tell me?
This book is a project you and I decided on a long time ago. It's a special project. It's filled with wonderful surprises. Just come and sit with me and I will help you to see where we are going. You must not feel guilty to change your mind about things. Life is about experimenting. If a creation is not working, it's okay to let it go. Try not to hold on. There is more to create.

Someone suggested an exciting idea to me today. Shall I follow it or not?
Yes!

It's scary doing things all by myself.
I know, but sometimes it's necessary. We each have a path to follow. You have to follow your own. This is important to teach to others. We have too many 'followers' and not enough 'leaders' on the planet. It's time you became a leader.

Did we know each other in a past-life?
Yes. We were very close friends. That is why you wanted to come into my family in this lifetime. The Karma is very intense and has been difficult for you at times, but you are doing great.

Good-bye, Poppa.
Bye, Sheree

♥ ♥ ♥

Earlier in 1999 I put together a CD called Transformation and a friend suggested that I create a workshop based on my CD. This was what my grandfather was referring to when he said I had to be a leader, not a follower. The conversation helped me feel better.

I asked my grandfather for proof that it was him that I was communicating with and I was told that I would just have to trust him. I decided that I would do that because I didn't feel the information was hurtful to me, and as a psychic I have trained myself to trust my intuition. I felt it was my poppa, so I continued with our writings.

♥ ♥ ♥

3

October 16, 1999

Poppa, do you know things that we on Earth don't know?
There is a lot I am privy to but it's not always information that is helpful to your growth at this time.

Do you know if there is a way to be thin without diet, less food, exercise?
Yes, it's having control over your mind. The mind says, "food equals fat." If the mind did not say that and instead said, "food equals energy," the more food the more energy, things would be different.

It can't be that simple!
Darling, things are simple. People there make everything complicated. You are conditioned to believe that everything needs to be hard. You are taught that to achieve you have to work hard. Here, in spirit, we learn 'easy' is the true way. Animals and birds are led by their instinct. Humans make it difficult because their thinking gets in their way. In truth, it's simple.

The people who eat and don't get fat believe food doesn't equal fat. Diets teach people that food equals fat. This belief is so deep that it overrides other concepts and becomes the dominant force.

Is there something I can do to the pituitary gland to change its information?
   Everyone's pituitary gland is perfect. The people's minds have to be changed.

How can I make myself a hypnosis tape with just a simple message?
   I don't know why you want it to be a tape or difficult. Each bit of food produces bits of energy. You love food. All food is turned into energy. Fat is all burning at a perfect level. Then you load emotion and belief on. That changes thoughts to:
   If I eat now, I will get fat.
   Belief equals result.
   Change in belief equals a new result.

Poppa, what else do you have to share?
   Love is number one. When you are walking and talking in love, all life is a mystery. All life is wonderful. When you are walking in fear, all life is confusion–confusion and fear. This cripples the person and stops their growth.

   Fear is not healthy. Fear is a way to avoid facing the truth. Truth cannot hurt. It's a definite and not something to fear. We each know the truth inside and it's always presented to us. Life is not an obstacle. It's not to be handled with fear. Meet it head-on with no apprehension or doubt.

Do you hear our thoughts?
   The energy of thoughts…energy is seen in shades or colors of the thought. Anger is red. Different types of red denote the level of anger. Joy is blue dancing light. Ecstatic is brighter. Each vibration of light is a thought.

Do you have all medical answers now?
I understand what happened to my body. I know the abuse of my thoughts on my body. I realize that bitterness and anger corrupt the body like wood that is burning. The longer the fire burns, the more our thoughts burn away at our body (wood). The result is decayed wood (body).

This week I correlated the origin of the sore throat–the fear stuck in my body from my tonsils being removed. Does everything stick in the mind and body?
There is nothing that happens that just dissipates, having no effect on the mind or body. Laughter affects the body. Sadness is in the body. But fear is the most dangerous thing for the body. It blocks the energy flow through it and becomes lodged, as you discovered.

Does everyone have fear lodged?
Yes, we all have memories that are lodged in the body. But release from the body is not enough. The mind has to know the origin of the fear, then it can be released.

Laughter is great! It's a medicine rarely used by man. We are afraid to be in a place of joy. The keeper of happiness is a person who retains youthfulness. That is a free spirit who sees life as a journey of discovery.

Is there anything else I need to know?
Teach. Teaching is a direct correlation to healing. Remembering knowledge and expressing knowledge, then clearing the knowledge, has to be taught. You are a teacher, Sheree.

I know, but it's hard to get things together here.
That's an excuse, feeling that it's hard is like fear. It immediately puts a wall up and says, "If you don't work hard, then you can't have what you want." Bull! Things are easy to achieve. Things are simple. You make it a struggle by using the word, "hard."

When you have me write things like this, my mind automatically wants to eat.
That's because I push you into the fear zone, the place you don't want to go. Food is a response to suppress that feeling. It's very simple. When you touch the feeling it's there in your face. Take a deep breath and see how relaxed you feel. Keep breathing and then the peace to the body will come.

Poppa, should we move? Is there a better house for us now?
The beach home awaits you. It will show itself very soon. This will be the right home for you. It has perfect energy. You'll have everything you desire. You will live on the beach. You will be happy.

When will we find this home? We have to decide very soon if we want to renew the lease.
I know. Remember each event leads to the next. There is no time. Be patient. Everything is in perfect order. Thanks for coming. We'll talk soon Sheree.

4

October 19, 1999

Hello, Poppa. How's everything with you?
It's crazy here right now. All the people are ready for a big event. The energy is very high. The weather is changing. The people will make big moves and it will affect everyone. The planet is going to be transformed. It's very exciting. We know this information.

Is this about the so-called Earth changes and disaster?
No, it's not so-called – It is! The weather will change. It will not hurt everyone. The ones that leave will be okay. The ones that are left will be changed forever.

You are scaring me. Will I stay?
Yes, my dear, the work you have dreamed of doing awaits you. Everyone will be changed. They will need your help more than ever. You will be needed and will receive tremendous joy.

In what way will I be changed?
That's not up to us. It's up to you. The changes are for the betterment of mankind. So you would have to look at them positively.

Is my family – our family safe?
Not all of them will be left on Earth.

Will Scott, Justin Andrew and I be okay?
Yes, you will all be together.

When will this happen?
It will happen in the year 2000.

At the beginning or end?
It will occur in the middle of the year.

Is there anything I can do to prepare?
Yes. Get all your work ready. The important things need to be together. The important papers need to be organized. The pictures you want to keep, diaries, etc.

Is St. Augustine, my hometown, safe?
It will be safe for a while, but then things will change. You will be told. Don't worry. Life will be good in the New Millennium.

You say life will be good. It doesn't sound very good...
Remember 'good' to one person, is a 'disaster' to another. For you, it will be wonderful.

Is my life planned out?
In a way the map is set: the players, the acts and the scenes. The words do change, but overall the map is in play the way you wanted.

Is this true for everyone?
No. Some people don't want to follow a set map. They want to flow with life as it comes up. Some numb themselves to their map through abusive substances and do not listen to their inner yearnings. Others are afraid and hide from their paths. That's why a lot of your responsibility will be to help them remember. Then they will open to the deadness. They will awaken to themselves and be free to follow their paths.

How much of the play can be seen?
It depends on the person. The way I lived my life, I wasn't too awake to my purpose. I didn't challenge myself enough and I am sad about that now. That is why I have agreed to work with you, to continue my work that I should have done on Earth.

What happened when you died, Poppa?
I realized immediately I was out of my physical body. The sensation was very familiar. I saw things in vivid color, brighter than on Earth. It was beautiful. I had a thought and it appeared. It scared me! I never realized how quickly thoughts could materialize.

The amazing part was the lights–the lights around everything–colors beyond what our eyes can see. "Where am I?" I thought to myself. Instantly, I heard music playing. I couldn't move. It engulfed me. I felt my heart expand. I cried for joy.

I then found myself in a rest area. I was taken care of, fed, and given time to adjust to my new surroundings. I didn't stay very long. I remember it was quite beautiful and similar to a cabin I visited in the mountains. I recall there were people with me.

After a few months in your time, I was ready to explore. This is when your Uncle Eddie, grandmother Katy, and my brother appeared. The whole family welcomed me home. They helped me to become familiar with my new surroundings. The people appeared how I remembered them but after a while their physical appearance was not necessary. We were all energy and love.

Is there anyone in Power?
Not in the way you see Power. We are all one. We are still separate and one. We each follow our mission in the same way as on Earth, but not for the same reasons.

What does that mean?
Well, on Earth motivation is for material things a lot of times. But here, it's for pleasure simply because it's our own creative expression, our own creation, the gratification and fulfillment of being a creative being.

What do you create?
I sew, I sing, I write, I read, I feel, I make love, I am 'one', I am 'everywhere'. There are no limits to what I am and can do.

Thank you for coming. We'll talk again soon.

♥ ♥ ♥

2003

It's always scary to me when people talk about Earth Changes. It's hard to see them as positive. There has definitely been a new energy in the air since we entered the new millennium. I write this at the beginning of 2003.

We are at the brink of war. Our nation was the scene of a horrific terrorist attack on September 11, which brought us to a trembling stand still temporarily and shocked most other nations as well. Many people are receiving immunization shots to protect against the threat of warfare via deadly diseases and chemicals which could be airborne or added to drinking water supplies.

Our nation is in the grips of the worst economic decline since World War I. The world is experiencing an increase in the number and intensity of earthquakes, weather changes, floods, tornados and fires. There is a sense of urgency in the air. I felt it the minute I woke up on January 1st this year. I knew I had to work hard and complete the projects I had begun.

My grandfather talked about seeing Eddie, his son, and Katie. Katie was his wife, my grandmother, whom I called Nana. Eddie was my mother's brother who died suddenly at age 52 of heart disease. He was a wonderful uncle to me.

My Poppa never married again. I asked him why he never did and his reply was, "I had the best. There is no need for another."

5

October 26, 1999

3:30 a.m. - *Lately my mind has been very active with all the things I need to get done and I have been waking up early every day. I have just put together the covers to my CD's and tapes and am working on my own 'Inner Child' issues. My day life is action-packed with home schooling Andrew, my eldest son, taking care of my 2-year-old son, Justin, as well as studying, healing and attending to the needs of my clients.*

Poppa, I'm having trouble sleeping so I decided to write to you. Is Nana with you?
Yes, she is always in my energy, but not the way you are thinking. We have a great respect for each other. Our connection is not intimate. We are colleagues at times. We share memories as souls who shared a path.

Would you want to be married to her again in another life?
If that is needed, I would. She is a great woman. It is not always necessary to play the same roles. It has not been decided which roles we will have again. She is very busy learning on this side.

Why hasn't Nana come back to Earth?
That is not necessary. She doesn't have the need to do that at this time.

Is Uncle Eddie near you also?
Yes. He is always with me. We both loved you very much. We are always around you, yet we are together, yet we are alone.

Why are people taken from Earth before they are ready?
That can't be answered in simple words. It's a way that the soul can evaluate his progress. There are many ways to grow. The greater growth can often not be limited to the time on Earth. We have to know that the soul needs to be free and if we are not growing on Earth the way the soul needs, it will be taken.

Can you see my future?
Yes, I can often see the direction you are going. I have observed the many different areas that you are here to learn about. Your soul sometimes works in one area more than another. Right now, you are growing personally as well as spiritually.

Can you see anything that would explain why I can't sleep right now?
Sometimes the body doesn't need sleep in the normal way. It can, however, be beneficial to the body to rest periodically throughout the day.

Poppa, for some reason I feel sad.
I know. I can feel your state of mind. Sadness is not a bad emotion. It's healing. Touching the feelings that arise as you experience an emotion can help you grow tremendously. They are a measure of where you stand in regard to your life. Sad emotions can help you open up which is healthy.

But, I feel kind of lost, too.
You need to examine that state of mind. Feel the feeling, then say, "When have I experienced this emotion? What is the origin of this lost emotion?"

I felt it when Nana died. I am starting to look at all that inner child pain.
It is all a wonderful part of your future. The way we release each emotion so that we address the behavior we are having is to ask ourselves questions. Where is our anger coming from? What needs are not being met? Each part of the unveiling can take you to the truth. Each memory is released and the freedom is so complete that the message keeps you going on and delving deeper.

Where does sadness come from? Loss brings sadness. Is the one leaving sad? Yes, in the sense they are attached to you and feel sad because of your sadness.

When Nana died, I missed her closeness.
That was an inner child feeling.

I seem to be feeling some kind of guilt, but I can't be sure why.
It's a known fact that guilt can be destroying. Your mind takes a mistake and turns it into blame. Then blame destroys self-love which destroys worthiness.

When were you guilty? Who isn't guilty? The flesh has memories of guilt, times that you went against your true inner feelings or couldn't stop the negative behavior. The repercussions are lessons. Without the experience, there is no lesson.

Don't we need to feel guilty sometimes to stop us from behaving a certain way?
If we are all guilty, then what allows the world to go on? Guilt destroys. How can this be the way?

But if you don't feel guilty, then how do we have remorse and the desire to not do "it" again?
By trying to be the best person you can be every day. By recognizing that no one is perfect and by loving yourself for your imperfections. Then you will understand the imperfections of others. For without the inner acceptance, there is no peace for humanity.

You are right! How can we get those messages deep in ourselves?
The experiences you have each day take you to this understanding. That is why everyone is your teacher. Bad things are not bad things. They are there to show you who you are and to teach you that "imperfect" is okay. Learning your lessons is very important.

Bye, Poppa. Thanks.

♥ ♥ ♥

During the time I started writing these conversations with my Poppa, I was receiving weekly body work and massage. A lot of my beliefs of unworthiness and my fears were based on my childhood experiences. Everything that happened to me was not only in my mind, it was also in my body, especially the sadness and fear.

I remembered during one of my sessions this week that I had such fear when I had to go to the hospital to have my tonsils removed. The fear was lodged in my throat. The reason I was so scared was my grandmother (Nana) had died in the hospital less than a year earlier. I thought I was going to die too.

♥ ♥ ♥

6

October 28, 1999

At this time in my life, I was experiencing a lot of anxiety over money matters. There were so many material things I wanted yet I felt my past was keeping me poor. Lack of money and lack of love is what I experienced growing up and I never felt anything I did was good enough. Somehow my experiences of lack as a child was keeping me stuck as an adult. So I decided to ask Poppa about this.

♥ ♥ ♥

Poppa, it's hard not to believe lack exists. Help me to understand manifestation.
Sheree, it's quite clear, you see things all around you—the birds, the insect, the trees, the ocean, the mountains and people. We are all manifestations.

Yes, I can understand that, but what about lack in the world?
Lack is a display of lack in our thoughts, a universal acceptance of good and bad, rich and poor.

How do we change this thought?
You have to change your way of thinking about miracles. Miracles do exist. You are a part of a deep miracle. From sperm you came into a body. That is a

miracle. Then the miracle became reality. You believe you can breath. You believe you can cry. You experience this every day.

How can I manifest wealth?
There are many ways to look at wealth. Do you think other people would perceive you as wealthy?

Yes, Poppa, I know other people may perceive me as wealthy but we are living on savings. Our finances fluctuate from month to month. I would like to have more money than we need for a change.
That's a matter of perception. What if I say, "Here's all the money you desire." Would you believe me?

I don't have it in my bank account right now
I know you think that. The thought creates the reality.

I'm not just thinking it. I know it.
Again, a statement of knowing, which is even more powerful than thinking!

Poppa, come on...
Sheree, it's clear. It's not that difficult.

How do I think something differently if I know it isn't true?
Once again Sheree, you know it, another definite!

This is very frustrating!
Okay, say I said to you, "*know* that you have millions of dollars. *Know* that the more you spend, the more you will have. *Feel* that you have millions of dollars."

How can I *know* it, and *feel* it?
You just do! There are no "but's," and no "I'll try's".

24

What should I do when reality hits? We can't spend money that isn't in our wallet!
　　Reality is a very interesting subject for another day. Good night, Darling.

♥ ♥ ♥

2003

I felt tired after this conversation. So I just went to bed (per my diary notes). Now, in 2003, as I read back on this time, I realize that some of the material things I wanted then are not as important to me now.

There are times when I feel my thoughts still keep me stuck and money doesn't flow like I want it to, but I catch myself and realize that God wants us to have abundance. This thought makes me feel better. This is a truth written in the Bible. God said over and over, "Believe in me and all things will be given unto you, great health, riches," etc. I'm allowing faith to guide myself a lot more lately.

♥ ♥ ♥

7

November 2, 1999

Hi Poppa. It's been a few days since we last talked. I feel like I am at a different place from the other day. Lack is still being presented. Why is that?
Lack is a very funny word. It can mean so many things. It's representative of a state of doing without. What are you really without this moment in time? You have a roof. You have food. The kids are well. Lack is in anticipation of a so-called event that could happen.

What other event could happen? Could you get a phone call from ten new clients that need your help? Could you get a call that someone has left you a lot of money? Would then your anticipated "lack future" change? It certainly would.

You cannot base the future by a mindset. Eradicating mindsets changes your future immediately. You may not witness them as quickly as they change. Yet they have because you changed the past, present, and future by claiming your worthiness to receive. You may not see it because you are still set on reality.

Speaking of reality, in some people's minds, you and I sitting here talking would not be reality! Would the whole world see this as truth? Yet it is truth, just like the past, present, and future is all taking place at the same time. Just because the understanding isn't there, it doesn't mean it's not true. Reality of how you see your world makes each person's reality different, but everyone is in the same world operating from a different perspective. You have to ask what you want your reality to be?

I want to fulfill my life purpose and enjoy a great future with my children and husband, in a beautiful home, without worry.
That seems really simple, Sheree. Why don't you just surrender and allow the events in your future to unfold? Know that they will. Do not hold onto the thought of how they will occur, just follow the yearnings you feel. Each day you will be lead. It's very simple.

Your path and mission were determined before you came to Earth. So now relax and enjoy everything that is presented to you. Enjoy the surprises, the magic, and just let it unfold.

Can you give me a hint of something exciting coming up soon?
A cruise–a wonderful trip.

That sounds like fun. What else will happen?
You will receive a phone call that will change your world. It will make you very excited and on a high for months and months.

Will I ever be famous?
There is no doubt.

Are you aware of the inner child work I have been doing, Poppa?
Absolutely. We are very impressed with your bravery and your willingness to fight to overcome the old child restrictive fear-based beliefs. It takes a true warrior to go into battle to fight limiting "ideas." You are a great warrior who has a memory that causes a lot of inner

turmoil. Fight your demons, wipe out your enemies, and love from your soul–your true essence. Let go of anything in your way; words, ideas, or people.

You can love without attachment: "Should's", "have to's" and "need it", are all lies. "Should" represents guilt, "have to's" refers to obligation, not necessarily desire. "Need it," represents lack. Back to the beginning. Not bad, eh?

Love you kid.
Always, Poppa

8

November 5, 1999

At this time, I was still receiving a combination of energy work and full body massages weekly. In each session, images and thoughts would come to mind for me to cope with and release. I felt relief when I acknowledge my feelings. At times I would cry to release; at other times I would take deep breaths until I felt better. Some of the memories that arose were from my childhood.

In other sessions, I had past-life memories. In one of these lifetimes, I saw myself lying on a battlefield unable to move. It felt as though I was shot in the left leg by a bullet. The therapist massaged my leg, and I actually felt her taking out the bullet. My leg began shaking during this session.

Forgiveness was the only emotion that brought me peace–the forgiveness of myself and the people who hurt me in those lifetimes.

♥ ♥ ♥

I feel very sad, Poppa. A lot of past-life memories flashed before me while I was receiving a massage today. At one point, I saw myself as a witch who was killed for working with herbs and spells.

Memories have to be released. You cannot do your work until the past is healed, because it's a block in your growth. The 'you' of today is not separate from the 'you' of yesterday. The only thing that separates is your belief in separation. When you are experiencing pain, it's in every time zone. The identification with the present makes you feel separate, but you are not.

The way to handle all the emotions is to realize them, not to deny them. In each day the message is clear. Now is all time. So if you are being tortured, the memory is in your whole body when it's recorded in your mind. Release has to take place mentally and physically, as you are finding out.

Of course it would make you sad. When you have spoken your beliefs in many places, you have been ridiculed, killed, or hurt. You cannot deny these things took place. Your initial reaction was to be angry at the old woman because she gave people herbs and did spells that allowed you to be killed. Yet, what did she really do? She did what she believed was right despite the ramifications. Should she not have helped people? See, Sheree that is the question.

If you have come to help people, should you stop yourself? You know now in 1999, you have come to help people. But if you don't do your work, your mission, what else do you want to do? Can you deny who you are? Yes, they can kill you for speaking of your beliefs, but you already know that. You've experienced it in many lifetimes.

Is it different now in 1999...are we safe?
Yes, in the way you are thinking, but death is inevitable. When you come to terms that death will happen, you will know there is nothing to fear. It doesn't matter how you leave Earth. One way is not

any better than another. The fear is what the body registers. The memory of how you died gets lodged in the body and mind.

Do you feel sad when you leave Earth?
In a way, you feel everything and yet you feel nothing. You are sad for the people who are hurting that you left behind. You are thrilled to be where you know you belong. You are frustrated that you didn't accomplish more. You are happy you came to Earth. All emotions take place at the same time.

Am I still holding back on my purpose?
No, you are exactly where you are supposed to be– healing the old beliefs from the beginning of time. You are much more than your body. Yet your body takes on all that you take on—beliefs, fears, doubts, negative thoughts, anger, and guilt. This is all recorded in your body. Because you are having bodywork and massage done, you are releasing these characteristics and behavior patterns.

How long will it take to release the lodged behaviors?
You will know when you are there. All your cells will rejoice and you will feel completely free. It can happen in days, weeks, months. The process is important also. Enjoy the process. Think of it as a lamp bulb which was burning out and now you are replacing it with a higher voltage. It will burn cleaner, brighter, at optimum level. This is a body that has unplugged from the restrictive beliefs. The celebration will be magnificent among us and there in you. You are almost there. Keep up the good work! Bye for now, Sheree.

9

November 11, 1999

Poppa, I have been given the opportunity to teach for the College of Metaphysical Studies. What do you think?
It's so wonderful, Sheree. It's a very prestigious opportunity. It moves you in the direction of your mission to help others. We are so proud of you. You should be, too. You have worked very hard to earn this gift. You will be able to help others understand themselves as metaphysical beings.

I can't express the joy we will experience as you complete what has taken eons in the making. Many blessings will come to you. Already the way has been paved. All you have to do is sit back and let it unfold.

My throat has been bothering me again today.
We know. It's the battle within, the battle for you to fight. The new year will free this energy and you will proceed in a new way with help. Get ready for fireworks, great celebrations, and the end of the millennium, followed by the beginning of the new. It will be the time for people to surrender and fulfill their deep inner missions and to rise above being prisoners. The past will be seen in a new way. Grasp all the opportunities. Surrender to the whole picture.

In each of us is a sunshine spark that is enlightened. In each is a clear joy and an honor of our truth. When we come into the new light, the message will be clear: There will be no turning back. The new millennium has arrived, the dawning of Aquarius.

Our work together is to help mankind grasp their fundamental right to freedom, a freedom they have not experienced before, the core of all they hold dear, their 'being-ness' and their oneness with their God-source within. They will have recognition of balance, oneness and love, where all people are created equal. Equality is not just a word, but a belief and a knowing.

We all have the ability to receive this information and the work you will be doing will move people in this direction. I will be very proud of your involvement and your schools will be a big success. There are so many unbelievable, amazing, fantastic miracles coming into your life.

Blessings,
Poppa

♥ ♥ ♥

The opportunity to teach here in Florida for the college was a total surprise. I was at Cassadaga, a spiritual community, and I arrived late to go in the stores, but in time for their monthly dinner. I was sitting with my friends and a man came up to me and said, "have you heard about the College of Metaphysical Studies." This took me by surprise because a few days earlier the thought of going to school had been strong. At the time, I couldn't imagine what I would go to school for so I dismissed it.

The man gave me a brochure which I took home and read. After some thought, I called the school for additional information. The president, Dr. Daniele, spoke with me and answered all my questions. We had a wonderful discussion and he invited me to meet him at his college in Clearwater, Florida.

When we met, he asked me to be a teacher in my hometown, St. Augustine, which meant I would receive credit for teaching as well as for home studies. I was very excited, so I asked Poppa about it.

During the time of these conversations, I had a constant tightness in my throat and sometimes I found myself coughing. It would come and go, but I wasn't sick. When I was working on fears and past-lives, the cough was present. I never discovered what it was and it continued to persist for a few years, but then finally disappeared.

♥ ♥ ♥

10

November 16, 1999

During this time I was busy trying to overcome my own self doubt. Even though I seemed confident to others, inside I felt very fearful.

There were so many things I wanted to achieve in this lifetime, yet I felt scared that I would fail. I intellectually understood about God, but I had not really internalized my faith.

I lived in fear of failure. I pushed myself to accomplish goals, yet I never had that sense of fulfillment. This probably stems from my childhood need to please, and inner feelings of not being good enough for my father to love me.

♥ ♥ ♥

Poppa, I'd like to talk more about fear.
It's kind of like our situation, Sheree. You know I've left Earth, yet you know I am with you. The veil is there between us like a curtain in a play and you can't see the characters behind the curtain, yet you know they are there. When you can't see the characters or the future, you will allow your mind to get fearful. You permit your thoughts to bring doubt to what you want. Doubt comes in many forms: negative thoughts, all-encompassing fear, procrastination, etc.

When you know that I am here; that I have gone nowhere, you will then realize that death–the greatest fear of all–is an illusion. It sets up the world play and underlies everything to be afraid of. If you remove your fear of death, you remove fear from your life.

Yes, but what if you are okay with death, but just don't want to be crippled or hurt physically?
Sheree, you are perceiving suffering as bad. What if I say people are disabled in life by their negative thoughts? What if I was a runner and broke my leg and had to run with an artificial leg? Even though it was harder, I would be able to show mankind that nothing is impossible. Which would have the greater impact, the fact that I was a great runner or my ability to continue to run despite my so-called disability?

You are right about that, but sometimes "disabilities" are not that much fun.
Each person's disability is their own Karma. If you are supposed to experience a physical disability in this lifetime, there will be nothing you can do to avoid it. Staying stuck in your fear will not stop it from happening. It will just stop you from enjoying your life and will fill your mind with worries which will cause your body stress, etc.

There are some things people must experience. On a deeper level each person knows that everything that happens to them was set into motion before they came to act it out on Earth. All the rehearsals were practiced over and over on this side–the stage, all the characters were in place, and all the sets were designed. The "actors" (people) are just playing their scenes every day. The "life play" is over when you leave this Earth.

Your job as human beings is to let each scene be the best performance you've ever done. Fill each act with your joy, enthusiasm, confidence, and love. Then you will enjoy each day.

Thank you, Poppa.

11

December 5, 1999

Hi, Poppa. I realized that I have a protective wall around my heart that doesn't believe in love! Why is it so hard to open up?

Sadness has a big effect on our consciousness. We take the messages and interpret them as true. If it continues, we adopt them as our truth. So we play out these messages over and over like a tape on replay mode.

To release our bondage to the past, we must be willing to face the hurt and the sadness, to feel it, to address it, to be it, and then we must forgive it and let it go.

This is the process you are involved in right now, Sheree. We each have to go through the process. It's like being in an underground tunnel. You go in not knowing what you will find. Each step can get you deeper into your pain (the mud), but as you continue trudging through, facing everything head on, eventually you will reach the end of the tunnel and would have crossed over the misery–to freedom.

I'm looking forward to being free. What can I expect?

Be patient. The light will be so bright at the end of the tunnel…it is love. You will be in total light.

But why do we have to experience the sadness in the first place?
You wanted to. You wanted to lead others out of Birth and Rebirth cycles so you chose to personally know the pain of rejection, loss of love, and unhappiness . . .

I don't want to experience it anymore. I want to love and be loved. I want to experience my Divinity.
I know Darling, and you are moving well through the tunnel toward your Divinity.

When will I be free?
Time has no relevance. Just know you have a lot of help from this side. Be patient and you will discover miracles happening everyday.

Is it possible for everyone to be free?
Yes, if they choose. As you know, it's no easy task facing the past. It's easier to forget than to heal. The work you are doing is painful, yet the most important for your soul growth. People have to want to change. Desire equals results.

Thank you, Poppa.
Don't worry, you are way inside the tunnel and are on the way out.

Know we love you always. Love and kisses.

12

December 14, 1999

Dear Poppa. Do you miss being on Earth?
There are things about being in an earthly body that are wonderful. We tend to see it as a hindrance but when we leave we realize how wonderful human flesh is. We could touch, feel, talk, walk and run; we could feel our heartbeat while making love; we could touch our lover and feel our lover's skin–what wonderful sensations! We could enjoy a small meal and feel satisfyingly full inside; and we could taste and smell delicious meals.

These are just a few of the marvelous experiences to be had on Earth. I, however, don't miss the eternal struggle of fear and negative thoughts. It's wonderful to know all is right, and all is taken care of.

The books I'm reading say we are God and God is us. We are not separate. This is so different from the feelings and thoughts we have learned.
Remember, thoughts can be changed. No one is stuck with their thoughts. New information is always arising to disprove original information. We each have to adapt our thinking as needed.

You are Divine. This is a fact. By not believing it, that doesn't change it. It just limits you. Why would you want to limit your ability? Just believe it is true.

Then, if it's true that our abilities are so great, we could create a world. We can have anything!
Yes, Sheree, it's greater than you could imagine. There is no limit. All unhappiness could be wiped out if you align with God within.

How do we do that?
You stop believing negative thoughts, doubts and fears. You only listen to the thoughts that align you with God. For example, right now you want to publish your children's stories and you are unsure if anyone will publish them. You have doubts about the stories. You have doubts about your writing. You have fear about rejection. This is not the truth. It's a lie of your limiting self. Your higher self knows the stories help children to know that metaphysical experiences happen all the time, and they are natural and wonderful.

Do children need to know these things?
What happens if you listen to the limiting ego? Will you get your book published? But what happens if you see yourself as divine, unlimited. Can God get your book published? Absolutely!

Could it happen soon?
In an instant! Which do you want to align with; the limiting self or the unlimited self?

When we leave Earth, do we then know we are Divine?
Some do and some don't. If they hold onto their beliefs, they limit their experience in this dimension. If they allow the truth into their consciousness, they realize a lot of what they learned on Earth is false.

So dying doesn't free us?
It just frees us from our physical bodies but it doesn't always change our perceptions.

Do you study or take classes?
Yes, in a way we do. Each experience is a class. In this dimension we continue to experience. Not the same way as on Earth, but we are constantly growing and changing here as well.

Shortly after I died, I was assigned a helper and he gave me choices of things I could do. I decided that one of the things was to help the people of Earth. This is why I am writing to you.

Thank you, Poppa.

13

December 26, 1999

Hi Poppa, this is a day I'll always remember–it was your birthday! Happy birthday!
Thank you, Darling. Birthdays are special times. As souls we see being born as a very special event. We want to come to Earth. It's very exciting. So to celebrate life is very special.

You probably already know why I am writing to you. As you know, I am conducting a dream study which involves a lot of past-life research and which has me a little frightened.
Yes, I am aware of your research and your struggle is my struggle. When you feel fear, it makes me sad. I feel sad that you see knowledge and adventure as scary.

It is hard not to be scared. What if something hurts me and I die?
Don't you teach your clients to have faith! Yet, you find yourself struggling with faith. Why is that?

I know, but I don't have faith in my protection.
Sheree, this is something you have to develop–your own faith. Sometimes doing something that you are scared of will give you faith. As long as you stay stuck in fear and avoid what you are afraid of, you will remain afraid.

Are you saying I have to try and do the things I'm afraid of?
    Yes, that is exactly what I am saying. Please remember that you have some very wonderful helpers on this side.

Will you help me?
    As much as I can. I know that you think you are alone, but you are not. Each step you take in developing your consciousness is a joyous event. You move beyond your fear.

I've been doing a lot of reading lately in *Friends of God* by Neale Donald Walsch and I know it's no accident I'm reading this book right now. Is this true about God? Have you met God?
    It's true in the sense that by having a friendship versus a fear of, will be the way to open your heart to love. I know love. By knowing love, I love God. God and I are one. There is no person to meet. There is just love energy. God is not found as human. God is not found as animal. God is human and animal. God is the essence of everything created.

Poppa, weren't you disappointed when you died, to not meet God?
    Sheree, God and I are one. I met God.

But weren't you disappointed to see that God wasn't a person?
    At first, but then I understood that I wasn't really a person, I was everything, which helped me understand that God is everything.

Please describe what it's like where you are.
Rolling green hills, crystal buildings, sparkling clear streams, sky of beautiful colors, many schools of knowledge, trees, lakes, oceans and rivers.

Do you sleep?
I replenish my energy through many things.

Have I ever gone in my sleep or meditations, to where you are?
Yes, many times.

Why do I not remember?
It isn't necessary that you remember. But if you desire you can come and remember with intention.

I know we all have a spirit guide on the other side that never leaves us. I haven't seen mine.
He will take on any form you need. He has no form. He is an energy. You have traveled many journeys, many lives together. He is always with you.

Will he be with me on my night travels?
He will always be there. You can trust in his protection.

Thank you, Poppa. I love you.

♥ ♥ ♥

During this time I was recording my dreams. I wanted to uncover my past-life memories, as well as direction in my life. I would ask a question by writing it down before I went to sleep. At times I would just ask, "What do I need to know?" Then I would often have a very insightful dream.

The day after this conversation with Poppa, before going to sleep, I asked to know about my soul desires and to know God and the dream that ensued placed me in an airport.

I was traveling to England, I thought with my husband, but he was nowhere to be found. I started calling for him, but he didn't answer. Moments later, I was in the waiting area and all of a sudden a spirit appeared. She was very tall and looked extremely powerful. She moved toward me and was crying. And then she said in a commanding voice, "Stop painting a rosy picture of your relationship with your husband." The woman was very upset.

I was petrified and wanted to runaway so badly but my feet just would not move. I was trembling and straining to make my feet listen to me. I woke up, soaked, chest hurting, and bed covers all over the floor.

A few days after the airport dream, before going to sleep, I asked to open my heart to love. In my dream, a beautiful young lady appeared before me. She said her name was Rachael.

As we sat and talked, she told me I was her mother in a past-life. She explained that during this past-lifetime, her father had been married to someone else for many years. Then I met him one day and it was love at first sight.

We maintained our relationship for several years and a daughter, named Rachael, was born. Then one day, he said he had to leave. He had to return to his wife even though he didn't want to do this. He was unable or unwilling to offer an explanation and said only, "I'm sorry I didn't meet you first." A last kiss and he was gone forever. Rachael said I was devastated and took my own life.

I awoke at 4:04 a.m. feeling extremely sad. I felt as though I had actually lived the events of my dream. In addition to feeling sad, I was experiencing a deep pain in my heart and heaviness on my chest.

There have been many dreams that were extremely upsetting. In one dream, I saw myself as a human sacrifice. I was a Mayan Princess. In that lifetime, it was an honor to be a sacrifice. I was shocked I would do such a thing. I was experiencing two lives daily. During the day I handled my responsibilities, and at night I lived a very active and sometimes surprising past-life. I found it very difficult to maintain a balance. My grandfather was my sounding board. I could always go to him and we would talk it through. He was like a spiritual counselor to me.

♥ ♥ ♥

14

December 27, 1999

> *Because of the dream work taking me into past lives and the memories that were being evoked as a result, I was full of anxiety. Even though I felt this way, I still was being driven by an inner part of me to continue. I had to break free of my own fears to progress in my work.*

♥ ♥ ♥

Poppa, fear has been a big issue with me lately. It seems so many of my dreams have contained elements that I find difficult to deal with. How do I get over it?

I've said it before: fear is a thought. The things you are thinking are creating your fear. Thoughts of fearful things bring anxiety and stress.

I understand that, but I know that what I am afraid of a lot of times is real.

You don't change the truth by denying the things that are real. By being afraid of them, you stay ignorant of them and in fear.

Are aliens real? If so, please explain about them and what they are doing to us.

Yes they are. You have been in contact with other realms for a long time. When you are a sensitive soul, you radiate a light that draws other energies to you. This energy transmits through the cosmos.

The aliens can see you and consequently they have been in contact with you. They watch, monitor, and teach you, which they have done for a long time. They have never hurt you. Do not worry over this because you are well protected. You are not alone.

I understand that, but I'm not popping in on them the way they pop in on me in the dream state.
Yes, but in the dream state you also drop in on many places uninvited.

I don't have too much confidence that they haven't hurt me. Why don't I remember what they do or say to me?
Sheree, you didn't want to remember. You protected your life and wanted your visits to stay secret. You needed to stay balanced. The rest of the world wasn't ready to accept you talking to aliens. You knew that. For your own protection, you asked not to remember.

You say all this but what if they did hurt me and took my eggs and implanted babies in me like the other people who have been interviewed claimed?
That is not something you should worry about. You are fine. You have already spent time with them. Did they hurt you?

No, but what do they want with me?
They work with you and always have. They are not around to hurt you, only to teach you.

I have trouble believing that. One part of me wants to believe it, the other part is not so sure.
I understand this uncovering has been a shock and I have been aware you felt betrayed. There are so many levels to God's kingdom. There is so much you do not

understand. Just stay open the same way you stay open when you speak to someone on the phone. Reserve judgment.

Are they visiting everyone?
No, they're only visiting the people who have a special mission in this world. Your purpose is linked with theirs the same way as my mission is linked with yours.

I've read in many stories that they hurt people.
Sheree, don't people on Earth hurt each other? Aren't people killing each other every day? They are similar. They have their bad "aliens" and their good "aliens." Not everyone has been hurt. Some aliens are truly concerned with our planet and are here to teach us and lead us.

How do I know the ones working with me are good?
Well, are you fine? Are you growing in knowledge? Are you bruised or hurt?

I want to believe the ones that visit me in my dreams are good, but I'm afraid that I'm being naïve again just like my past-life memory of being a human sacrifice as a Mayan Princess. I went along with that blindly.
You did not, you believed the same way as the others that the afterlife was the real life and Earth is a temporary abode.

Okay, assuming they have no plans to hurt me, then why are they around me?
They want you to understand that they are here to help. That your mission on Earth is very important and that they are real. Your being afraid of them doesn't make them less real.

When did I choose to work with aliens?
Before you came to Earth.

I do not remember making that choice and as far as I'm concerned right now, I want to know what they want with me, why, and who they are.
You will receive all these answers in due time. Please remember you are protected. You can trust me on this.

Thanks, Poppa. I will bear this in mind as I think on this. I love you.
I love you too, Sheree.

♥ ♥ ♥

In my dreams, I became very aware that I was talking to aliens. In the dream, I seemed to be okay with the conversations, but when I woke up I was shaking.

In one dream, they seemed to be all around my bed. I found myself saying, "can you please make sure Scott wakes up better this time?" They said, "yes, but we have to go now." Then I was jolted awake by a loud noise.

I grabbed the bed and held on while I scanned the room for aliens. Happily, none were present, but I couldn't stop shaking. I was able to focus enough to think about my dream and a shiver ran up my back as I remembered the words, "This Time." What did I mean, "This Time..."

My mind started racing. This meant they had visited me before! Then panic set in. What were aliens doing to me? I kept the dream all to myself, but I had to consult my grandfather about it. I, however, was not comforted when my poppa told me the aliens were real.

I did not want to accept what he was telling me. It was one thing to be a psychic and draw on the resources of metaphysics, but to say I was working with aliens in my sleep was just too far a field for me to be comfortable with and therefore, I tried to shut it out.

In the year 2000, shutting them out became impossible. Just before I went on the cruise that Poppa talked about, a client gave me a book about alien abductions. Without even opening the book, I had a detailed dream which showed flash backs where I was in communication with aliens since childhood. I was devastated and I felt betrayed. In the dream, the alien took the form of a large dog. In my anger, I yelled at the dog, "leave and never come back!"

I woke up crying and tried to talk to my husband about it, but he did not want to discuss it. I grabbed the book and went up to the deck to try to gather my thoughts.

I had many questions and I felt very sad. Who could I share this with? What had the aliens done to me? Did I really want to know? I opened the book and started to read. I couldn't believe that in the first chapter it was written that aliens often appear as animals so as not to scare children, confirming my dream. After I completed the book, I decided I didn't want to know anymore.

As I write these comments today in 2003, the subject of UFO's has surfaced again for me, but this time I do not feel as anxious. Clients have been showing up to confirm the existence of aliens. One lady came to see me and said she had observed strange lights in the horizon over the ocean. I also dreamt a big spaceship came out of the ocean and dolphins were jumping all around.

Just a few days earlier, another lady came to see me, and she wanted me to regress her back to when her baby was a few days old. During the regression she described aliens in the room and was crying out that they had her baby. I tried to keep her calm and asked what they were doing.

In between her tears she said they were holding the baby upside down and she couldn't move. I asked what happened next and she said they gave the baby back to her. I told her to ask them why they had the baby upside down. They replied that the baby had stopped breathing and they had to work on it. I was shocked and so was my client. The aliens saved the baby's life. She felt a lot better after the regression and so did I.

♥ ♥ ♥

15

December 29, 1999

During this time, I was studying Intuitive Development through the College of Metaphysical Studies. As I completed each course, I would then teach the course.

I earned my Masters degree in Metaphysical Studies in 2000. I would discuss some of the subjects with Poppa. He showed me that God's love is truly unconditional. It was hard for me to accept this concept because many different faiths portray God as cruel, revengeful and angry, and teach that we should fear Him.

♥ ♥ ♥

Hi Poppa, what can we expect in the next year?
We can expect some battles of the forces between light and dark. As light becomes brighter, it shows where there is darkness. There will be a lot of people who see the world in chaos. Yet through chaos the eye is peace. So it's nothing for you to worry about. There is no more past. People will not be able to hold on anymore. Beliefs will have to change. The ways things are done will change. People are in for large awakenings.

How will this affect me?
　Your work will be very intense. People will need your help. You will show many people the light and you will be very happy.

I am glad to hear this. What else can you tell me?
　I know you will be pleased to know you will publish your books. Also, you will talk to a lot of people and they will listen. You will still have time for your home life and it will greatly improve.

When I do my Sitting for Intuitive Development course, I hear a force telling me how much I am loved. Who is it?
　It is God.

Wow! Sometimes that is so hard to believe. Why would God love me so much?
　He loves you not for what you do…but just because you are you.

But sometimes I know I could be nicer. How can he love me then?
　He loves you always. It isn't based on being good or not. It is just so.

That's hard to argue with!
　I know. Just accept that it is so.

I'll try. Good night, Poppa.

16

January 9, 2000

5:41 a.m. - Poppa, I had a dream that deeply troubled me so much that it woke me up. I dreamt I was taken to an unfamiliar house. I never saw who took me there and I did not recognize its location. Once at the house, I found that someone I cared about had died and I was told I needed to be okay with death. How do you become okay with death?

It's very sad, Darling. Death is sad for the people left behind. You lost your grandmother when you were very young and I lost my wife. We both shared a very deep pain. I lived the rest of my life without her and felt very alone.

Love is a very powerful bond. We both loved her near us in the flesh. When that was taken away, we felt we were all alone. That pain makes us very sad. It hurts. You were crushed. But as you know now, there is only a curtain that separates you from me. At times the curtain can feel very thick, but in reality it's very thin. I am with you. Love doesn't end in death. In fact it greatly increases.

As I am writing this letter to you, my solar plexus is hurting.

It's the fear in you, the fear of letting go. That part of you that has to hold on because, if you let go you will fall apart or you will be disloyal to the person that died. That is, of course, nonsense. The people who die want you to know they are okay. They don't want you to be in pain. In fact they want to help you. But in your pain and sadness, you have trouble being open to the fact the person you love is never really gone. They continue on in another place.

Your Nana has always been with you. When you think of her and close your eyes, you feel her love all around you. That is what you felt as a child and it's still what you feel right now.

You are right. I do feel her loving presence when I close my eyes and think of her.
Then remember: death is nonexistent. Physical sight is the only thing that is gone. But you can visit your Nana anytime you wish. All you have to do is ask before you go to sleep. I love you, love doesn't change when you don't see me anymore.

Why must people leave Earth, especially when they are so young, like Nana was at 49?
On a soul level they have completed what they came to do. It's just like when you leave a job. There is nothing left to do–it's over. Leaving Earth is the same thing.

Why did Nana have such a short assignment? I needed her here with me.
I needed her also, but for her soul growth and for ours, she was also needed on the other side. She opened the door for you by giving you the knowledge of the unseen world. She showed you that so-called Death did not exist. She was there every time you needed her and she gave you comfort. You never felt alone. She has always been watching over you. Love doesn't die.

Sheree, look at us. We are writing to each other. Have I left? In what way are we not together…physically? Well, we have been physically apart a lot. I lived in

New York and you lived in California. Distance is distance; New York or here, where I am now; what's truly the difference?

Physical touch, I guess. It's sad not to have physical touch from the people you love when they are gone.
It's time you realize the place you are at is temporary. You are borrowing a body to be grounded on Earth for a designated period of time, to fulfill your desires in physical form. Your real home is here on the other side.

Thank you for your visit, Poppa. I always feel a little better when I can talk with you about things.

♥ ♥ ♥

My grandmother (Nana) died when I was three years old. She went into the hospital and never came home. We lived next door to her and Poppa, and I saw her every day. One day she was there, and the next day she was gone. I was so overwhelmed with grief that I couldn't sleep. My mother told me the doctors put me on drugs to help me sleep.

Then one night I saw Nana standing at the foot of my bed. She looked as I had remembered her and she was smiling at me. She said she came to visit me to remind me how much she loved me and to tell me she would always be with me. She also asked me to take care of my mother for her.

In later years, my mother told me that on this particular night I ran into her bedroom screaming at her that she was a liar. She said I told her she lied when she said Nana was dead because Nana was still here and had been in my bedroom with me. She said she didn't know what to say to me at that moment. I certainly was happy to see my Nana and from that day forward, I was able to sleep calmly and have always felt her presence in my life.

♥ ♥ ♥

January 20, 2000

My grandfather would visit almost every week. We didn't talk much at that time and I must admit there were times I didn't like him very much, especially when my step sister and I had to share a room with him on vacation. We fought about how long Poppa spent in the bathroom...typical teenage girl stuff. Poppa was always around and it wasn't until I was older and had my first child, Andrew, that our relationship got closer.

❤ ❤ ❤

Hi, Poppa. It's such a joy to be able to speak with you.
Thank you, Sheree. I am always pleased when you are joyful. Our bond and our missions extend beyond time and our love is continuous, even if you didn't think much of me when you were a child in this lifetime.

What do you have to share with me?
Sweetness, each person on Earth is an extension of each other. If you stretch your hands out to each other, one leaves off, the other one begins. We all need each other. You begin to see everyone is important to the whole. The link of all mankind brings us to the whole...the whole being God. So each link has a piece of God in it. That's why we are all special.

A lot of people, including me at times have trouble believing we are special.
> That is very sad. But as I have told you before, that does not stop it from being true. When you accept that you are special and that you are loved, you will be able to trust that you are protected and that nothing happens to you by accident. Every step you make is right for you. Each of us has a divine plan for our life, and each person's plan will lead to a divine conclusion. Just enjoy the journey.

Fear can be so powerful that it stops us from trusting our Divine plan.
> But Darling, fear...how can that be good if it cripples you, if it stops you from enjoying your life?

It isn't stopping me from enjoying my life, but sometimes it seems so overpowering and I just feel compelled to listen to it or I'll die.
> Oh, so fear can kill you, or doing what you really want will kill you!

People listen to fear like it's a warning not to do what they want to do.
> Sheree, in the caveman times fear was a warning of possible harm. But in modern times fear is different. It can refer to rejection, for example. What will happen to you if you send your book to the publisher and you are so-called "rejected?"

Nothing, but I may be sad.
> Does that kill you?

No, but it can hurt our self-worth.
> Why is that?

Because they didn't want to publish my book so they must feel it's not good enough.
Does it kill you?

No, it does not kill me.
If you are afraid to move forward in your life and you are letting fear stop you, then you will never know, for example, if your book will get published. Fear becomes a lie. It's based on all the belief systems that keep you stuck: "Nobody will want to publish it, I'm not good enough, I'm not a writer, why would anyone want to read it?" These are all negative thoughts that you have to eliminate.

I'll try, Poppa.

♥ ♥ ♥

A lot of our fears and belief systems originate in childhood. The true healing work is to change the beliefs that limit you. This has been my goal for many years. At times it seems there are many layers to our beliefs. We uncover one and it leads to another, usually rooted in childhood events and past lives.

As I review my conversations with my grandfather, I realize now that fear comes up a lot for me, even with my metaphysical background, I was still dealing with a great deal of anxiety.

I am working extensively on reprogramming these beliefs through self-hypnosis tapes and creative visualization.

♥ ♥ ♥

18

January 28, 2000

11:56 p.m. - Hello, Poppa. It's very late as I begin to write to you tonight.
    Hello, Darling. I'm here.

I'm always amazed at how quickly you are able to respond to me.
    You have to realize our connection is immediate. You write to me, and my consciousness focuses on you. It's like a thin veil between the two worlds–you just lift it and I appear.

I have a few concerns. I was talking to a man tonight and he said his wife had to fight Satan in her sleep.
    Yes, Sheree, that is possible because Satan is very powerful, but not more powerful than God. Calling on God and light protection will always guide your way. Satan is real. He's real in the sense that evil thoughts create evil actions which bring disharmony into lives. So Satan is constant where disharmony abounds.

Satan and his evil are certainly scary, Poppa.
    I know, Darling, but what have you been learning about fear? Fear is negative. The opposite of fear is love. Protection is love. Fear has no place where love is the guiding force.

Why must we deal with Satan?
Satan is a reminder. A reminder to mankind that if you constantly entertain negative thoughts, if you take your mind to hate, evil, drugs, murder, you take your mind to Satan. People always have the choice where their thoughts can go.

We are the keepers of our thoughts. If you think about yourself as protected and loved, this will create peace. Peace and love create balance. So being afraid of moving forward is not the answer. The answer is to keep your mind on joyful, loving thoughts, then Satan can't live in your mind or your life.

Why is it difficult for us to want to stay positive? What makes us go back to negative thoughts that upset us?
Comfort, familiarity…these are the reasons. They are voices that we have heard our entire lives saying: "We are not good enough, something bad is going to happen, if I'm happy, something will happen to take it away."

All these messages are so ingrained in us that we just accept them. Then we listen to them and allow them to rule our lives. They determine our happiness. The only way for things to change is by thinking positive and refusing to listen to the negative. Delete negative thoughts from your mind by thinking, "I am completely safe, only good things happen to me. Everything is always a blessing in disguise. Nothing is totally bad. I always seem to be at the right place, at the right time."

Thanks, Poppa. I'm getting sleepy. We'll talk soon.

❤ ❤ ❤

This conversation with poppa helped me feel more relaxed. It helped me to realize that Satan was not a real entity but is created by negative and unloving thoughts. I realized that if I kept thoughts of love and faith there would be no room for doubt, evil or fear.

❤ ❤ ❤

19

February 12, 2000

My husband and I, after 15 years of marriage, decided to go for counseling. I had reached a point in my life where I was very unhappy because as a couple we had drifted apart and were living more like roommates than lovers. I wanted this to change. I needed love in my life. I also wanted our two children, Andrew 6, and Justin 3, to grow up surrounded by love. My dreams were even showing me I needed love. I felt through counseling we could reconnect and become closer.

♥ ♥ ♥

Hi, Poppa.
Hi, my Darling. You have been going through a very tough time, a major transition. You have changed all your Karma. Many people are involved in your transition. You are well protected. Don't be afraid.

Wow! Boy, you can say that again. What is going on?
Well, the play you set in motion has been completed. You are changing on multi levels. This is a time to rest, recoup, and celebrate. When someone changes his destiny, we are thrilled. You have decided to be free. You realize now that having no love is more painful than having love and losing it.

Love is the most special energy. It can move mountains. It can clean rivers. It can stop pain. You are very blessed at this time. All energies in the universe are supporting your transformation. We are all dancing. This time is the greatest in your life. We will teach you many wonderful things.

Fear has no place when you ride the train of love. We have heard your cries, we have felt your pain, and we hear your desires. You have survived the darkness. The rest is joy, happiness, and love.

That is wonderful! I am really ready for that.

Poppa, the more I learn from you and experience, the more amazed I become. I have complete faith now that the spirit realm is very real. I knew it, but there was still some doubt at different times.
Of course it's real. We are constantly aware of your thoughts and needs. We wait patiently for breakthroughs and celebrate every triumph you make on this side.

Life on Earth is not easy. There are many tests, but most of them are chosen by you. You picked all your experiences and took part in all the plays, to arrive at a place of complete harmony.

It's a brick at a time. Each brick eventually builds a house. You cannot build the top of the house before you build the foundation. Fear is like loose bricks. They can tumble and break. Faith, strength, and trust, on the other hand, are the foundation for a strong house. You are building one now. The old house crumbled because it was built on fear. Sheree, I am very proud of you. I am always watching over you. Don't worry Darling, love is yours to have.

20

February 19, 2000

Dear Poppa, I'm feeling a little lost and sad this morning.
I know, my Darling. We are always aware of your feelings. Feelings come to us in colors. We can see the colors you are radiating.

Sometimes our emotions can block us. Right now you are out of balance. In search of growth you are learning of new realities and have delved into a new realm. With growth comes discomfort. When you work through your emotions, you will find peace. Just enjoy the process. It will be all right. I promise.

I feel so uptight.
Of course you are uptight. Your so-called reality is changing. You will never see things the same way again. This is not a bad thing. The way we see things is limiting. It is not necessarily the truth. You are opening yourself to new realities. It's normal to feel out of sorts. It's okay, though. You will be able to handle it. Don't worry.

Thank you. I'll try to let it be okay.
Sweetheart, you are so blessed. All I can say is you will be so happy. Just hang in there. I love you. You have a lot of protection.

♥ ♥ ♥

Sometimes my conversations with Poppa were short. He was the refuge I sought out, even if only for a few moments. This day, I woke up and found myself crying because I had two boys and no girl. I realized that in the past lifetime where I died of a broken heart and took my own life, I hadn't been able to love my little girl. I probably made a decision from that life to never have a girl again because I felt guilty for abandoning her. I also feel I made a decision not to ever love that deeply again.

♥ ♥ ♥

February 20, 2000

Hi, Poppa. What will be my lesson today?
I have come today to help you see how your life is being directed. You have chosen life paths. In each path there are courses to be taken, kind of like courses to get a college degree. You take life courses to develop your awareness. One course leads to the next. It's the same for everybody. Some have very difficult courses, some choose to take it easy in this lifetime.

You are on the difficult courses right now. They are about facing what is really important to you. Are friendship, love, peace and joy important to you? These courses challenge you to uncover all your beliefs on these subjects. You must test yourself and face your truth, without judgment or guilt of others, or yourself. It is not an easy task.

Meditation is very important to help you sort out the really important answers to the test. Make the time to study and learn and then address the answers to this course very carefully.

Thank you, Poppa.

♥ ♥ ♥

I started meditating when I was twenty-three. I remember being very nervous and apprehensive when I first started meditating. I thought the spirits would say bad things to me, but instead, I received love, acceptance and peace.

♥ ♥ ♥

22

March 5, 2000

During this time, I had a friend who owned a school. She was expanding the school to include an afternoon program. On this day, it was the opening of her new center. It was a very interesting day and I met a lot of talented spiritual people and later became involved in teaching classes there.

♥ ♥ ♥

Hi Poppa. I sense your presence in the room.
That is good Sheree. I think today we will discuss sensitivity. The world looks upon being sensitive as a bad thing, yet it is an asset.

Look how you can feel my presence here with you. You are very sensitive and because of this you have compassion. You can feel others' feelings. You can even hear others' thoughts. You absorb their feelings and make them your own.

Many people at today's opening were striving to develop. The room was filled with a lot of energy. There were a lot of lost souls and a lot of enlightened souls. It was a real celebration because when you bring the light to the dark it is very powerful.

Will the people in darkness wake up to the light?
Sheree, everyone will wake up in some lifetime. Some people though, may require hundreds more lifetimes; while others, tomorrow. It's all in Divine Plan.

Is everything in a Divine Plan? Is it necessary to be at war, or for young children to kill other children?
Yes, in a way it is. What is the growth that comes from war? We learn war is not the way. We learn that the pain of killing–even in the name of your country–is still pain. We learn how children are in pain. It forces us to make changes, and find solutions. Without examples, we have no growth. So these violent events are teaching us a great deal.

Others may not see things that way, Poppa.
That's true, Darling, and that is why war still goes on and why children still kill other children. But know they will eventually see things with "light." When that time comes joy will reign on Earth.

Sometimes it seems as though joy will never reign. It seems too good to be true.
There are many things we never thought would happen. In my time who would ever have thought there would be talking robots and spaceships. So, why is it so difficult to imagine today what the news of tomorrow will be? There is nothing out of our reach. Look at me communicating with you! Some would say this is impossible, yet you and I know it is possible. You wait and see...joy and love will come to Earth.

I understand. I just hope love will reign the Earth sooner than later.
So do we all, Darling. So do we.

23

March 16, 2000

Reading back through my journals I found that I had been complaining about a lack of stamina and motivation. I see that some days I barely had the energy to get out of bed.

I read in my journal entry of March 16, 2000, that I asked for the knot in my solar plexus to be removed. In the dream that followed, I was shown that all my fears had been stored inside me: the fear of divorce, the fear of poverty, and the fear of going hungry.

♥ ♥ ♥

Poppa, I feel you calling to me to write.
  Yes, I have been calling to you. I need to tell you that some big changes are coming your way. You are going to experience some changes in your body and in the vibrational frequency you operate on. The process may feel scary, but don't worry. It will be fine after the adjustment is made. We are altering your chemical composition so that we can prepare you for the changes. So it could feel uncomfortable for a week or so. Please don't panic.

How do you mean uncomfortable and why do I need this adjustment?
Darling, the work you are becoming more involved with requires more from you than you are currently prepared to give. You are releasing your past Karmas and freeing the energy that has been blocked. This is good, but this change will make a great difference in the way you feel inside. It will feel unfamiliar and your equilibrium will be scattered.

However, if you will be patient, you will adjust well. We are with you. This is the reason for the increase in food and your inability to diet right now. So, give yourself a little while and be good to yourself during this process.

Thank you for the advance warning and explanation, Poppa. It's good news to hear there is nothing medically wrong with me. I will do my best to hang in there.

I would like to know more about the place you are. Tell me how you spend your day and what you do for relaxation.
Well, I do various things, such as dance, sing, paint, mix with some wonderful people, play cards (although, it's a little different from Earth because we know what the numbers are on all the cards). I take walks. I can smell, see, taste, and touch everything instantaneously. I also study literature, but I don't need to read to study. I see the information just by touching the book.

You can read a book just by placing your hand on it. How wonderful, if I had that ability I would probably overdose on information.

How is Uncle Eddie, and will I ever be able to communicate with him like I do with you?
>Hi Sheree, I'm with your Poppa today. I'm Uncle Eddie. I wanted an opportunity to tell you I have missed you very much and I send you my love often. I see you have grown up to be a wonderful person. You are doing a lot of work to help mankind and you should be very proud of yourself. You were a lovely little girl and have grown into a very special spiritual lady.

Thank you Uncle Eddie, I am so pleased to have a chance to talk with you. I miss you, too.

Poppa, I've noticed lately my psychic ability has changed. I am better able to communicate with entities on the other side, and I have been called upon by a number of people here to do this. Is this something I will be doing more often now?
>Yes, there will be more people coming to you now because the people on my side want to let their loved ones know that they are still with them. They don't want them to grieve unnecessarily. We are all one, whether here or there.
>
>Love is timeless. When we pass over, we are so free and at peace. I relate it to like waking up in paradise where we are surrounded with love. There is no sadness or pain here. Then we see our loved ones struggling, hurting, and brokenhearted, and we want to say to them, "we are here for you." Please know that I will never leave you!
>
>We need people like you as channels for the bridge from this side to yours. We communicate through you, the same way as I can write to you.

I've become keenly aware lately that the spirit world of angels, guides, unicorns, fairies, mythology, and other universes, etc., genuinely do exist.
You are right, Sheree. God's kingdom is vast. It holds more mysteries and surprises than you could ever imagine. Waiting for your mind to confirm all this information would be impossible. There has to be a point where trust, mystery, and surprise lead and you just watch it unfurl. Enjoy the mystery.

Not all information will or can be available to you while you are in physical human form. The mind could not possibly grasp it all. Just know it all exists. Every folk story, mythology, custom, ancient belief has its elements in truth.

Thank you for coming. I wish you Peace and Love.
I love you too, Darling.

❤ ❤ ❤

In this conversation my Poppa helped me realize that the physical changes I experienced were normal for the mediumistic work I was doing.

❤ ❤ ❤

24

March 23, 2000

Hello, Poppa.
    Hello, Sheree. It's wonderful to see you researching Jewish mysticism. We have our own very rich heritage, just like the Shamans, Mayans, Incas and Native Americans. In all beliefs and religions there is a core of truth, the truth of creation, the truth of hidden information and deep knowledge.

    In your search you will gain valuable insights. This will enable you to see that one belief is not the exclusive truth. All beliefs contain truth when you dig deeper. You will discover that Judaism, not the limited Judaism taught in most temples, but ancient Judaism, is very close to New Age thought. Being that you are from a Jewish family, it is very special to me to see you learn about the Kabbalah and the customs.

I have been enjoying my studies: the different belief systems and customs are quite interesting. The other night, I had a dream about being given different stones to put on my coat and my totem animal, the horse. What did it mean?
    You are well protected and grounded in the energy of the Earth. All things have Divine Spirit.

Why stones?
Most stones are untouched and unaltered by man. They are pure energy with each being a manifestation of the many facets of the Divine.

Is the information in the Kabbalah accurate?
Yes, my Darling, heaven has many levels. There are many things to experience, and many ways to climb the ladder to awakening. The Kabbalah is a good route. There are many others as well.

How do you feel about Shamanism?
It's not something I have fully studied. There are many others on this side that can tell the miraculous joy and growth that Shamanism can bring. It's very ancient and has undergone many changes due to interpretation. It deals with transformation and freedom and is very much needed on Earth.

What about religion?
I was a very religious man. I loved the Jewish way of life and am even more proud being on this side because Jewish people were willing to sacrifice for humanity to teach suffering and help humans to gain compassion and love. The job of the Jew has been to educate, heal, and open the heart of mankind.

On this side, the whole picture is seen. We were chosen to be a light to the world. Just as the Incas and Aborigines and Native American Indians taught to work in harmony and balance with everything. Jews were willing to be the sacrificial lambs to help humans wake up to equality. Each religion, way of life, has a purpose. Just like each bird, mammal, fish, reptile and insect has a purpose.

Keep up the good work, Darling. We will talk soon.

♥ ♥ ♥

I had been working on one college course at a time. I enjoyed the challenge of the classes and I found myself actually living out the information, especially the courses that gave me exercises to work on each week.

♥ ♥ ♥

25

March 28, 2000

Hi Poppa. Can you talk with me now?
    Hello, Darling. Of course I can. In fact, I'm glad you have come to talk with me. We have a lot to discuss. You are in a place that is very hurtful for us to see. I know you are working through the pain and the scars left behind from your childhood.

    In life we have a lot put on our shoulders and in order to grow, we have to heal the scars of our past. You are engaged in very intense work and you need to lighten up and be kinder to yourself. Be kind to yourself the same way you would be kind to a friend who was hurting and needed someone to talk to. You are often there for others. Why not be there for yourself?

    Sheree, your marriage is in trouble. Consequently you are seeking help. I know you have met with a counselor, but uncertainty has not allowed you to be candid. It will be okay, she is the right lady to help you. Open up and share your feelings with her.

Okay, I will schedule another appointment with her and try to be more open. Poppa, will Scott ever heal his past and become the man I need?
    It's going to be a long haul. You have to be prepared. Childhood has a great influence on our life. When we are ignored, pushed aside, bullied and made to feel unimportant, then we have deep-rooted anger and low

self-worth. Even though we go to great lengths to keep it buried, when we least expect it, someone points this out to us either in words or actions, and the result is like an erupting volcano with hot lava shooting up, out and running down.

This is the accumulated debris associated with pain and scars from the past. Then something happens that forces it up, like you insisting on changing your marital lifestyle. Right now you are dealing with Scott's dirt and debris. There is so much rage buried inside him and now layers are being exposed. It's a long way to the root of the matter. You have to step away and not participate. His healing process is just beginning. You, on the other hand, have been uncovering your pain and scars for a long time.

I'm not sure I'm strong enough to deal with this. Our marriage has been going on like this for such a long time. I wish everything would be okay again and soon.

That's a normal response, but you have help. Lisa, the counselor, who is trained in this field, will help you through this. Right now, she is the stable foundation you need to help keep you in balance.

This is no fun.

I know, but it's necessary. You have to try, for the children's sake and for the fourteen years you and Scott have been together. I'm not going to push you. You have your own pains. It will work out wonderfully. Just be patient.

That's easy for you to say.

I know, and I'm sorry you are going through this. The pain and anger from his past are like dead plants he has been carrying around. They have to be pulled out for new ones to grow.

Having children is so much responsibility.
You are right, but no one is perfect and with the knowledge my generation had, we did the best we could. Your father had no nurturing as a child, so he didn't know how to love you. Your mother was filled with such pain in her marriage to your father that she just wanted to get away. In all that, you felt abandoned, unloved, and didn't develop good self-worth.

You are starting over yourself. Be very kind to yourself. It's a joy to see you heal. Don't get caught up in Scott's process. Let the counselor handle that. I love you Sheree.

I love you too. Thanks for coming and caring.

♥ ♥ ♥

My journal indicates that during this time, things were getting worse in my marriage. Scott and I were not communicating at all. I was feeling the need to end my marriage almost daily and I turned to Poppa for comfort and advice.

♥ ♥ ♥

April 20, 2000

At this time we were celebrating Passover, the Jewish holiday. During the holidays, Scott would buy me flowers. I really wanted tulips and told him, but I ended up with lilies. I was upset until I talked with Poppa today and he helped me understand the meaning of the lilies.

♥ ♥ ♥

Hi, Poppa. It's been a long day. Scott bought me some flowers today.
Yes, I thought that was interesting. You wanted tulips and made that very clear, but he bought you lilies instead.

I feel as though he really didn't care what kind he brought me. Do you know why he did that?
The lily is white like snow and pure like truth. It represents beauty and light.

How, Poppa?
Light is what is needed on planet Earth. There is a lot of darkness, fear, anger and hate. This all deepens the darkness. The lily is the light that grows out of the darkness. Always remember light is always there. It's there in the hugs you give to your children at night. It's there in the hugs your children give to you as they say,

"I love you, Mommy." It's there in the hello when you pass a stranger while walking on the beach, or when someone says, "I'm sorry for being rude. I'm in a bad mood." You see, light and love are both the same.

Are there other realms besides the place where you are now?

Yes, there are deeper states of being, but this is the only place I have been so far. The majority of souls, from what I have been told, are here.

If there are higher places, don't you want to go there?

All I want is to be one with the source.

Why do we have to be on Earth with all the temptations, density, and negativity before we can be one with God?

That is a great question. Our souls wish to experience life. We are forever experiencing joy and excitement to express our Divinity. Freedom to experience life brings such joy to the soul. In a way, our souls are like children, so thankful to God for the ability to have a body to laugh, run, play, and create. It's like billions of Gods all dancing independently, like the stars.

Will you reincarnate?

Yes, I will come back again. It's necessary. Everyone in this level comes back again.

Why is that?

Sheree, you know why. We have not yet completed all the Karma and the lessons.

Can you choose not to come back?

Yes and no, we can choose when we are ready to fulfill our missions on Earth, but not "whether."

When will you come back?
I don't expect to be returning for a long time. I have a lot of learning to do. I feel I don't need to take on a human body at this time.

When you went to Heaven, Poppa, was there a judgment time?
Not a judgment–it was more like an evaluation. You would perceive it as the teacher, at the end of the school year, looking at all the work a student has done to evaluate its worth and whether the student will advance.

When you arrive, without a physical body, on this side, you are aware of all you have been and participated in. All feelings are looked at, all actions are reviewed, all knowledge is recorded. In this evaluation you are not judged. You merely review and conclude.

The other night before going to sleep, I asked my soul what it needed of my personality. I dreamed "I" was sitting on the couch and my body was asleep on the bed. I saw it clearly and I realize now what the term, "out of body," means. My question is, "Who was the person that was sitting on the couch?"
That was you, the real you.

Was that my soul?
Yes.

If that was my soul, where was my personality, the character of Sheree?
She was asleep on the bed.

Are the body and the personality the same?
   Yes, they are like the character image. This is the character's shape…body, thoughts mind, all contained in one character.

If my character is sleeping, then who is doing the dreaming?
   The character.

That's confusing. If the character is asleep yet dreaming, then I was sitting on the bed looking at myself sleeping. Then who is the one on the couch looking?
   Sheree, your character in her dream, sees your soul sitting on the couch looking at her sleep. Your soul is always looking at the body, the character it's playing.

Well, I see now what you mean, Poppa. But now I think I will call it a night. Thank you.
   Good night, we'll talk again, soon.

♥ ♥ ♥

I have kept dream journals since 1994, but I was especially diligent about it from 1998 until 2001. I love dreams and now teach workshops on the subject. A number of my favorite types of dreams are flying, out of body, and lucid dreaming. When you are having a lucid dream, you realize you are dreaming while in a dream. By doing so, you can go wherever you wish. The awareness that we are more than our physical body is extremely powerful. There have been many books written on the subject.

♥ ♥ ♥

27

June 15, 2000

I haven't talked with my grandfather in a while. A lot has been going on in my personal life. Sometimes we are put through situations where we can't see the outcome. As a psychic, it's easier for me to read other people, than it is for me to read myself.

I had a friend...at least I thought she was a friend. She was going through a divorce and was calling me almost daily to talk. One day, she asked me to do a phone reading, long distance, with her sister. I agreed to do so. The sister and I talked and we did the reading, but I felt some resistance from her sister by some of the information that came up during the reading. Overall though, I thought it was a good reading.

The next thing I knew, I received an extremely nasty letter from the sister refusing to pay for the reading. I tried calling my friend to discuss this with her, but she would not talk to me. From that day forward she never spoke to me again. This was all very hurtful and confusing to me.

♥ ♥ ♥

Poppa, I know it has been a while. I've thought about it many times, but just couldn't get in the mood.

Sheree, I understand. There has been a lot on your plate, as the saying goes. We are well aware of all the turmoil you have been going through. Don't be discouraged, as I have told you many times. You are well protected. We have a lot of time and energy invested in our connection with you and it's important for you to maintain your balance. Energy can come in good waves or fractured waves. When you are balanced, our connection with you is stronger.

Why do you keep saying "we?"

"We" is just a metaphor for the spiritual unity up here. There are others that are helping my connection with you. It's necessary. So I say "we" because it is we.

Do I know any of these people?

Yes. Some you would know because you have spent time on this side. You have many friends here.

I've been through a lot with friendships recently. It's been difficult to trust others.

Darling, that is to be expected due to the situations you have come in contact with lately. We are not going to say it will be smooth sailing from now on, but we will say you have gone through a very karmic situation and you handled it pretty well. At times you lost your cool, but in all, you completed the karma.

Is that true even if it means an ending to a relationship?

Yes, endings are part of earth life. In truth there are no endings. But on the karmic earth lesson wheel, you completed it with your friend. You gave and that is the most important part. If others don't want to receive what you give, that is their problem.

You must always honor the truth and follow your own inner prompts. Others will follow what they want and sometimes their road is not the same as yours and that is okay.

That is hard to accept, especially when I treasure friendships and give a lot of myself in time and caring. This is the hardest lesson for me to learn: To let people go even when I love them.

This is difficult for everyone. Do not be so hard on yourself. Try to be a little more patient. We love you.

June 27, 2000

Hi Poppa, I really need to talk with you tonight.
I'm glad to talk with you again. I know things have been hectic for you. What do you need to talk to me about tonight?

The other night I dreamed that you were dying and Uncle Eddie was there and you gave me a black coat that you said would stop me from ever being cold. What did you mean?
It's very simple. Your life has been filled with a lot of inner turmoil. People often take your kindness and generosity for granted. You are a person who is willing to share your whole soul; others are not. The coat is a symbol of your protection. You should be well aware by now that Uncle Eddie and I are on your side. We came to reassure you that you are being protected by us on this side.

Thank you, I appreciate that. Sometimes my work and my beliefs make me feel very lonely.
I know, Darling. Stepping out as a leader is a lonely road traveled by few. You promised yourself not to buy into group consciousness and are willing to look crazy, weird, whatever society is going to call you. You have to be okay. This role is not for the weak or fearful. But as I showed you in the dream, the coat will protect you.

I want you to realize our connection is real and has been established over many lifetimes. You and I have work we have decided to do together. We were all there last night when you gave your talk. It went lovely. You were inspirational. We were all very proud. You have a lot of spiritual support.

Thank you, Poppa, and all who guide and help me. I am happy you all were pleased with my talk. It was a small group this time, so I was able to address everyone there. I hope my talk was able to help get them back on track again.

Everything light-workers like you are doing in the world is making a difference. It's important to keep on spreading the news. Small groups are much better than big audiences. A small group makes it easier to reach out to each individual, determine their area or areas of need and share information with them. It's the most important part.

No one is more honored than anyone else. Each is moving at his or her own pace within their comfort zone. There is no judge. The only judge on your planet is you. You (people) are the worst critics of yourselves, and always finding reason to fault yourself even when it was not your fault. You are not responsible for the decisions people make.

As a child you were made to feel responsible for almost everything. So you have to purge that part of your past from your mind. People act from where they are. Don't make it your fault, and don't try to analyze it. It's too draining. It doesn't change the fact that others have to live by the decisions they have made.

Keep the faith, as the saying goes, "Faith, that for every door that closes, another one will open." Be glad for change. It's refreshing and exhilarating and very necessary. Think of the weather. We need change. When it rains, everything renews and rejoices. The Earth is fed. We are blessed with healthy fruits and vegetables and the flowers smell wonderful. Rain in one's life offers the opportunity to renew, refresh, and begin again. It's God's reprieve. A new play can begin. Be okay with the rain. It's a definite needed part of life, growth, and happiness.

That was motivational, Poppa!
You are not the only one who can deliver a sermon.

What can I say to people who don't believe that I have really been communicating with you?
They are going to think what they are going to think. You or I can't convince them otherwise. Each has been given the mind and insight to know if something resonates with them or not. We can do nothing to convince them of anything if their mind is set.

There are many people who still believe we are alone on this planet and universe. What can we say to them?
Sometimes people need their beliefs for their own protection. It keeps them safe in a box. Nothing can move their box. But a day will come and that belief will be shattered and they will know that life exists everywhere, and that death is an illusion, and that "aliens," (other beings), exist and have always come to Earth since the beginning of time. And especially now that so much is riding on the work you and other beings on this planet are doing. To others they only see an empty screen, an empty universe.

But be ready, because the proof will be given to your planet and it will not be able to be dismissed, regardless of how the government and the medical establishment attempt to cover it up. Then the people like you will be taken seriously.

Movies infiltrate information in a form that the subconscious mind gradually accepts. The time is near that it will be told that many have had "other-being encounters." People will realize not everyone can be crazy. Just keep what happened to you in a peaceful thought because the experience is a blessing and not something to be afraid of.

I'll try, Poppa. At least others have paved the way for me.

Yes, there are many brave souls on your planet and they are to be commended.

Thanks for coming. I'm sorry that when I was a teenager I had so much trouble liking you.

Sheree, I had so much trouble liking you, too. But I grew up and so did you. I always loved you, even when you made me angry.

Boy, that sounds familiar! I hear myself saying that to Justin all the time.

Again, don't go back to that blame stuff. Move on. Don't take it seriously. Each event brought us to today and here we are, defying logic, yet together in this wonderful project. Who would have guessed?

Yes, who?

Well, let's talk again soon. Bye.

29

July 19, 2000

Weeks have gone by since I have written to Poppa. My world is changing. At the beginning of July, Scott and I had an appointment with our marriage counselor. At the end of our meeting, we were told our marriage was over and that I needed to be more honest with myself.

Due to our poor financial situation at this time, the counselor suggested that we live together like roommates. I was shocked to hear this. She did however, help me realize that I was deserving of more love and affection. I was now turning to my Poppa for support.

♥ ♥ ♥

Hi Poppa, can you talk with me for a while tonight?
I'm so sorry, Sheree, I tried to warn you in the dream. I knew you didn't understand. I told you that you would never be cold again. It was in my will. Being without love and touch in your life is being cold. For a long time, you have denied yourself these things. You can't make another human being be the way you want them to be. But you must not pretend to yourself that everything is fine with you.

Children are important. But what is crucial is the love you give to them and the love they see all around them, especially by their parents. This is not what your children see. They see a mom who is lonely and unhappy. Words are not necessary with kids because they respond to the energy in the room.

I never wanted to be divorced, especially since I came from a divorced home.
I am well aware of why you remained in an unhappy marriage, but that doesn't make it right. We have been watching you for a long time. Love is meant to be shared and demonstrated. Hugs and kisses and making love are normal human behavior. You are a normal human being. Scott, on the other hand, has elected to deny himself love and affection. He had a choice and he chose emptiness.

Poppa, I often hear a man's voice speaking to me in my head when I walk on the beach.
We know. He was sent to you to show you the love you wanted. He is in love with you and will come into your life soon.

The voice does tell me he loves me and he sounds sincere and very real. As I listen to him, I want to reach out and hold this man's hand, but a part of me is having difficulty believing what I have heard. I feel that it must only be my imagination.
I think I can understand the confusion you are experiencing, but what is the difference between listening to me and listening to a man in your head?

The difference is you are dead. Is this man dead too? He told me he can come to me now. How can he do that if he is dead?

Sheree, you've got to stop limiting your experiences and realize there is so much you don't know. There are many dimensions that one can be in touch with. People can connect also on the astral plane. This man is sending his love to you and you are picking it up from that dimension.

How does he know how to find me and how do I know he is right for me?
He already told you he will find you and can you imagine that someone who is showing you such love and affection on the astral plane wouldn't be a great guy for you?

Sometimes this all feels so unreal.
Yes, I can imagine it must, considering most of the world's population is deaf to what they can't see and touch in the physical realm. But just because it's in your mind, it doesn't negate the truth of the experience. You have been crying out for love and passion for a long time. Is it that hard to accept that someone heard your call? After all, it may look like we are gone, invisible, but we are not.

I guess my other alternative is to believe I am going crazy.
Yes, that's another way you could believe.

I don't want to think that.
Well, then it's important to trust what you are receiving and go with it, and soon it will all come about. As I said in the dream, you will never be cold again.

Thank you, Poppa, for helping me to be calm and patient in the here and now. Bye.

It's not easy for me to admit I have an imaginary friend. It all started several months ago. I enjoy a daily walk on the beach which is near my home. At first, I blew it off as the wind, but soon after, also during a walk, I had the distinct feeling that someone was holding my left hand. The hand was strong and supportive, but I was unable to discern anything further.

After he accompanied me on several other walks on the beach, he began talking with me. He said he loved me and was going to put his arms around me. Almost immediately, I began to feel warm. Sometimes during our walks I would tell him I knew he was just my imagination and if anyone knew I was walking on the beach with an invisible man, they would think I was nuts. He, however, was steadfast with his belief that he was real and expected to be entering my life.

We would discuss many things and sometimes we would dance on the cool damp sand. Even after many walks on the beach, he never told me his name. This unseen new friend made me feel loved. I couldn't wait to get to the beach to walk with him. At this point I didn't care whether he was real or not, I loved his company.

30

August 1, 2000

Hi, Poppa, Scott came home today and said he wanted to try our marriage again. I know you are aware of all this, but can you tell me why I have experienced such sadness through the separation?

For one thing, Sheree, in your type of work you must be able to understand the suffering of others. Secondly, you must be sympathetic and be able to appreciate the troubling circumstances other people are experiencing. And lastly, you have first-hand experience with your own personal pain and suffering, which will enable you to develop the sensitivity to be a deeper channel.

You are right, I do have first hand experience with pain and suffering and the whole situation has made me more sensitive and compassionate.

You decided before you even came to Earth that part of your mission was to help souls heal. You were given the experience of loss very early in your life. When my wife, your Nana died, it left you devastated. Nothing brought you comfort, not your parents, friends or toys. The only thing that helped was the visit from your Nana, and from that time forward you understood that life went on after death.

You always felt her presence, and in times of sadness she was always by your side. You often called out to her just as though she was in the next room and would be coming to see what you wanted. Other people need the same encouragement and you represent the bridge to our side that can provide the people with the answers they need. You don't have to worry so much about how or what will happen.

Sometimes that is hard to do; after all, it's only human nature to be curious about the future.
Yes, curiosity is healthy, but there must be surprises in life. Life is like a play. There are characters to study, a story line to follow and interesting twists and turns in the plot. So, the curtain is about to rise and the play to begin, so just relax and enjoy each act of the play and we'll worry about its ending when the time comes.

You are right, but sometimes it's difficult to be patient when what is just over the horizon could be very important and could result in drastic changes in our lives.
Just be patient Darling. Everything in due time.

Poppa, when I ask a question, do you instantly know the answer?
No, that is not the way it works. I go to school and I study, too. I learn better ways to develop my connection with you and how to better understand human nature. God's plan is greater than you could ever imagine. Therefore, it's so complex that I don't have all the information available at my fingertips.

I find myself drawn to ancient civilizations right now and, therefore, I am reading books about the Mayans, the Gurus of India, and the history of Stonehenge. Can you tell me why I find these topics of particular interest?
Yes I can. It's because you have lived lives in those places and times. Your inner self is pushing you to remember this knowledge.

What am I trying to remember?
You are trying to access soul knowledge by breaking away from logic and tapping into the unseen realm.

Is there anything else besides dreams that can help to access these memories?
Just keep working with the dream state and ask more definite questions and trust the information you receive.

Thank you for being there when I need you, Poppa.
Good night. I hope we talk again soon.

♥ ♥ ♥

In my personal life at this time, Scott and I decided to try again to make our marriage work. Yet most of the time, I was numb, scared and very untrusting of him. My dreams were filled with memories of other times which probably did not help my state of mind. I was always pushing myself to learn and do more and it was like I was being led to look deeper and to explore more because I wanted to remember everything I had experienced in my past lives. It must be the over achiever in me that causes me to feel I should do everything myself.

♥ ♥ ♥

31

September 1, 2000

We went on a trip in August that had a very strong impact on me. We were staying at a hotel in Mississippi and one morning I got up at 7 a.m. to take a walk. After the walk, I sat down by the pool to meditate. I asked, "What does my soul have to fulfill in this lifetime?" Then, I felt as though I was transported by the water to a snow-capped mountain where I was met by my soul. She said, "Come with me," and I sensed we were flying back in time. I briefly saw myself as an unloved child and then we went back in time further to a deeper pain. I felt as though I was a prisoner and my deepest sorrow was that I had not fulfilled my purpose in that lifetime. This lack of fulfillment weighed so heavily on me that I asked to leave.

I then asked, "What is my purpose in this lifetime?" I saw myself meditating with numerous other people. Then I saw that I was the teacher. I asked, "Where is this place?" The impression that came to me was the images were from the future. I understood that sometime in the future, I would be teaching a large number of people and my finances would be significantly better.

The trip was definitely strange. At one point, while in Tennessee, Scott and I were accused of being kidnappers. I was stopped by the police at *the hotel where we were staying and held until the FBI arrived. Apparently, Scott looked like someone who was wanted for kidnapping. They even questioned Justin and Andrew regarding whether or not we were their parents. I felt like I was having a flashback to the vision in which I was a prisoner. Everything turned out all right though and we were happy to get home without further incident.*

♥ ♥ ♥

Hi Poppa, how are you?

Greetings Sheree. I know you are experiencing a tough time. It's not easy to have faith. Faith is realizing that the so-called 'invisible world' has only good in store for you, and that where you stand right now represents only one small element of a much bigger purpose. Everything that happens is perfect for your soul growth and is in Divine order.

On your side of the curtain, it appears to you that you will have no place to live and no money to live on, but the true picture is unseen by you. The true picture is full of dreams come true and everything rests on how you want to look at it.

In everything you are doing, you have been guided by unseen forces. That guidance does not ever leave you. You need to make room for a new reality. The house you are living in no longer serves your purpose and Scott's work right now no longer serves his purpose.

I understand all this, and deep inside me I am trying to be positive, for that is the only way I can look at these changes we are undergoing. I know there is a reason for everything, but it's hard to be patient.

Right now, the thought of packing and unpacking is not too appealing to me. I would be a lot more excited if I was sure we would be able to move into an even nicer home on the ocean and Scott would be getting a great-paying job which would enable us to open our spiritual center.

Sometimes faith has to precede action. Through faith, action is perfect. It's in alignment with divine fate and purpose. Just hold onto your hat; the ride is bumpy, but you will arrive safely at your destination.

I guess that's all I can do. Why does everything have to be a struggle?

This is the way you chose it. Through adversity, struggle and lack all come to faith. It's a very old story. It's the story of history. Who says it's bad? It is only the fearful mind that creates negative thoughts and dramas which we are so quick to enter. Stay calm, you are loved.

♥ ♥ ♥

A few weeks ago after our trip, our landlord called to say she would be bringing a property appraiser to the house because she was going to sell it. She told us we had to move out by November. This news upset me terribly because we had lived here since 1997, and I had been happy there. I loved this house because it has a big backyard with a pool and a deck that faces the ocean. We considered buying the house, but she was asking too much money and at this time, our finances were less than desirable.

♥ ♥ ♥

32

September 22, 2000

Within a few days of my last conversation with Poppa, we found a beautiful, newly constructed home for sale quite by accident. We were looking at a rental house and while we were there we noticed a 'For Sale' sign on a house across the street. Although we did not have any money to buy a house, we thought we would go and take a look.

The house was completely finished except for the carpet. The deck looked out over a large pond and waterfall which was so peaceful and serene. Additionally, the house was only one block from my favorite beach, which meant I could walk to the beach anytime I wanted to. We liked everything about this house and, of course, it was even the right size for our family.

We looked at each other and we both knew we wanted this house, but we did not have any money for a down payment. We dismissed the thought and continued our search for a descent rental property. We lost count of the number of rentals we looked at, but none of them fit our family size and the new house kept calling to us.

We decided to go by the house again at night. We walked to the pond and there was the most beautiful sight we had ever seen. There were huge white egrets nestling for the night. There had to be almost 100 of these birds sleeping or getting ready to sleep in the oak tree. They looked like angels and for some reason I started to cry. I just had to have this house.

Scott did not believe it was possible to purchase it, so he kept saying, "we can't afford to buy a house, we have no savings and I only have temporary employment." It did not matter to me what he said because I believed in miracles and I was ready for one.

Within a few days my miracle came. I told my father, who lives in England, about the house. He listened but did not say anything. Then a few days later he called me and said something that totally shocked me. He said his heart told him to give me the down payment for the house as an early inheritance. I was so happy I broke out in tears. My miracle had happened. This was the phone call that Poppa had promised would come.

Within days we made an offer on the house and it was accepted. We were scheduled to make the move on October 31st.

❤ ❤ ❤

Hi Poppa can we talk?
Hi Darling. I am aware you are being well blessed at this time. Sunshine often comes out after dark clouds have lifted. You are moving into a new phase in your life. The woman who just came to see you represents the new phase for you. You are each giving birth. She is giving birth to a baby soon and you are giving birth to a new you…a trusting and loving you.

You can appreciate God's miracles now because you realize they are real and nobody can tell you differently. You went to hurt, felt pain, and surrendered in faith. You let go and let the universe do its magic and the rewards are still coming.

I am so proud of you. All you desire is coming to you. Your dreams are God's dreams for you. Just keep dreaming and allow your garden to grow. Let God continue to bring magic into your life.

Sheree, being a minister is right for you. Everything you have experienced will enable you to effectively minister to the needs of others. Accept and enjoy the blessings coming your way.

Mazel Tov on your new home. Love, Poppa.

33

October 3, 2000

Hi Poppa, I really need to talk with you.
Sheree, I know you are most anxious about this move, but try not to be. This move will be the best you have ever made. You will not be saying goodbye to anything. On the contrary, you will be saying hello to the 'new you.' The 'new you' has broken free from the past and free from your karma. You are now traveling the road of destiny along your life path. You should celebrate. There is magic in the air.

Shiloh means peace, which is why you were given the word in your dream. It's a wonderful name for your spiritual center and everything that is destined for you will now materialize. Congratulations! We are all celebrating for you. It was a lot of work but you broke the karmic spell.

Is this really true?
Yes my Darling, your life is now going to be magical as you help others break free.

Why am I feeling a little blue right now?
Part of you is ready to move forward to your new life, while a small part of you is still clinging to the familiar things in the past. You know there is nothing in the past to be concerned with anymore, but I know it's still difficult to step into the new without looking back.

You are beginning life anew with your family in a marvelous new home you never expected to own...a dream come true through a miracle. Your new home is in the most ideal location to provide you and your family the enjoyment of nature and serenity. Look only forward to the wonderful life ahead of you.

Can you tell me more about my new life? Are you privy to more detailed information about my future?
As I have said before, some things we know, many things we must wait to see what unfolds.

Then tell me something you do know about my new life!
I know that happiness and success await you. I know that you will be totally fulfilled with your work and life. And I know that the karma from your past is over.

I can hardly wait. Thank you for coming to talk with me.
I love you Darling, and am very proud of you. Keep up the good work.

❤ ❤ ❤

My grandfather mentioned that my karma was completed and that I had broken free from the past. I do feel something powerful happened to me when my father gave me the money so we could buy the new house.

I did not really believe my father loved me because of the rejection I felt by him when I was a child. I always felt he gave all of his love to my younger brother and that he preferred not to have me around. So when my father told me his heart told him to give me the money we needed, I knew he did love me and this made me feel wonderful.

I believe my father and I have known each other in many past lives and our healing was taking place in this lifetime. At this time there was a group of us who wanted to form a spiritual center and we discussed names for the center. In the recent past, I had a dream and was given the name of Shiloh, which means peace. Therefore we decided the center's name would be Shiloh.

We met once a week and drew up our By-Laws and applied for nonprofit status with the IRS. Scott, being an accountant, helped us with the paperwork. Happily, our relationship (Scott's and mine) improved as we focused on the new house and I was hopeful.

♥ ♥ ♥

34

November 14, 2000

Hi Poppa, it has been a while since we talked.
It's good to hear from you. So much has been going on in your life since we last talked. We have been watching it all unfold for you and we find it very exciting. God has been very kind to you.

I know I have asked you this before, but I have been trying to understand God. Can you help me to have more clarity?
God is all around us. The peace that you are starting to feel in your new home, magnify that a thousand-fold and that is what radiates around us. God is everywhere.

What about Jesus?
Jesus is a Love Energy. He was a person who came to Earth, but he returned to the Source.

Do you see angels?
Angels are the same. They are a type of energy that inhabits our energy field and they appear to be small specks of bright light. We all know we are surrounded in Love light. "Angel" is a term to describe the light.

I think I remember you telling me there are other places you don't have access to. Is that true?
Yes, we are aware there is an even brighter light where some have gone.

Aren't you curious to go there?
No Sheree, I have been very content here. I love my work and my studies and I have no need at this time.

What about in Nana or Uncle Eddie?
They are very busy too, Darling. We do a lot of things to help and comfort mankind on Earth.

What kind of things?
One thing I have been involved with is helping the atmosphere. I have almost learned how everything runs. It's a very complex system, what you humans call an 'Ozone,' is deteriorating and we are researching the problem. It's a good thing. I enjoy science.

I do not remember you ever liking science while you were on Earth.
Well, you have to keep in mind that while on Earth I had a work-karma to fulfill. I was a tailor, so that was my work-karma and now I can pursue my own interests and I love it here.

Poppa, as you know we have formed the Shiloh Spiritual Center. Is this the right path for me?
As you sit there, you know the answer to that. It's something that has been destined for you to do. It's going to be more magnificent than you can even imagine. Stick to your visions for the center and wait for the vision of the others to kick in and the center will explode in magnificence.

A man has chosen to join us. Is this a good idea?
You will have many others join as the years pass. The balance of male and female energy will be important to stabilize the center.

There is nothing for you to worry about. Everyone is coming to you as they are needed. Just let it evolve. It's like pregnancy; you don't stop the pregnancy to make sure the baby is developing properly. You must trust nature knows what to do.

The same is true for the Shiloh Center, which started with a nucleus of several seeds and now has begun to grow. The center is growing and developing and before you know it, it will have matured into a fully functioning spiritual center. Nurture it well because the center will become important to many seekers.

I feel a strong connection to nature being in our new house.
That is wonderful. You were created from nature and therefore you have a deep connection with nature. You and nature are one. Your heart and your emotions are both guided by it. The wings of the egret birds resting in your tree are the wings that you also carry on your back. They are unseen, but nevertheless they are there.

A lot of books talk about God's love for us. If God loves us, then why are we constantly being reborn and returned to Earth in another lifetime?
Why do you think this pattern of rebirths is not love? We enjoy returning to Earth in physical form to play. In a physical form, we have the freedom to explore and grow and play.

But, Poppa, it's not easy for people here.
Sheree, that is their own doing. They resist and see themselves as alone. But, as I have said before, no one is ever alone. They have allowed their emotions to be in control and thus these programmed thoughts are making them miserable. They need to change their mind set and then they will be able to change their life.

From my view, I can see the wonder, beauty and love on Earth and I know how lucky you all are, but as long as they see the world in a negative way, they will be miserable in their lives.

As usual it has been great talking to you. I feel a little tired now so I will say good night.
  Talk to you soon.

♥ ♥ ♥

It was nice to hear the encouragement from my Poppa regarding the Shiloh Spiritual Center. The Center was able to move into its first building in 2002 and continues to grow.

♥ ♥ ♥

35

November 17, 2000

Hi Pops.
    Hi yourself. You are looking much better these days. I am pleased you are losing weight.

I am too.
    You must not push yourself too hard, though. You have come a long way so go easy with the weight loss. Maybe you should coast a little, "sit back and smell the roses," as they say.

I have been trying to, but giving myself permission to relax is difficult.
    I know but it's necessary. On Earth people put so many rules and restrictions on themselves.

We have had rules since Moses received the Ten Commandments.
    I realize this, but who can really say they can follow those rules. You have a society today that does not follow them, and then feels guilty and unloved by God. Do you think that is what God wants? I don't think so. God wants everyone to feel his Love. Every-one should practice forgiveness because forgiveness is the only way to happiness on Earth.

This is all very idealistic, Poppa, but what if someone kills, should that person be forgiven?
If they should not be forgiven, then you are all guilty, for you have all killed. War is part of your history and each of you have killed in past lives. Your society kills animals every day for medicine, food, clothes and just for sport. Killing is killing, so now, who needs to see themselves as superior?

I get your point. So what you are saying is that we need to go by our inner rules instead of those imposed by religions and those from the past.
Exactly, find your own inner beliefs–the ones you can live with–then you will be free of guilt and able to allow God to love you exactly as you are.

♥ ♥ ♥

Weight loss has been an issue for me for as long as I can remember. I went on my first diet early in my teenage years. I would eat nothing all day and then have my dinner. As I look at pictures taken of me during that period of time, I can see that my weight was fine, but to me back then, I felt fat. This obsession grew worse as I got older. When I was nineteen, I was in a serious relationship that became intimate. I was so obsessed about my weight and it got so bad that most days I would eat and throw up, two to three times a day.

This behavior continued until I was twenty-six. Nobody in my family knew what I was doing. At that time, eating disorders were not openly discussed. One day, however, a friend, Christina, caught me and later gave me an article to read that really scared me into stopping.

At twenty-seven, I got married and learned hypnosis. As a hypnotist, I was able to make my own therapy tapes focusing on eating less and increasing exercise. I was able to maintain my weight and eat normally for the first time in my life. I did well until I was thirty-five. That year I elected to become a vegan vegetarian and a little later, I became pregnant with my first child.

During my pregnancy, I became concerned about getting enough calcium and protein. It was an unavoidable issue because every time I went to the doctor I was bombarded with information about the need to have the proper nutrition for the baby to mature properly. I found myself over compensating by eating nuts all day in an attempt to satisfy the protein requirement. In the end, when I delivered, I had gained 60 pounds.

My grandfather saw me after Andrew was born and mentioned he was worried about my weight gain. After two children and nursing for six years straight, I was starting to lose my excess weight.

♥ ♥ ♥

36

December 1, 2000

Dear Poppa, I decided to write to you because I am in conflict. I feel torn between the things I am committed to and obligated by, and the things I would really enjoy doing. What do you suggest?

It's not easy juggling your life, Sheree. You have young children that need your love and attention, so this is your most important assignment, if you will. A positive and happy mom is the best example.

Now, another thing you have to ask yourself is, "what will make me positive and happy? If what will make you happy is in conflict with your obligations, then you should honor the things which will make you happy.

You are right. I need to do some journaling and see what is most important to me and then make time for it. Thank you for listening to me.

You are welcome.

♥ ♥ ♥

I was doing so many things that I felt overwhelmed. I home schooled our sons as well as taught myself to draw. It was a juggling act to find time for family and exploring my creativity, as well as taking clients. Sometimes my conversations with Poppa were just to vent my frustrations.

37

December 27, 2000

Hi Poppa, happy birthday for yesterday.
Thank you Darling. We are proud of you.

Why do you say you are proud of me?
You are growing. It's easy to stay the same and do nothing, but you push yourself to be better.

Maybe that is a fault.
No, it's not. It's not comfortable and it can manifest as stress, but it's a good quality. Being comfortable and safe is usually the way a person lives his or her life. Challenging yourself to grow and learning new things makes the difference between great people and mediocre people.

I am not great, I am only an average person.
You are great to us. In the past, the church in the name of religion did not permit the people to explore their own ideas and greatness. So in the deepness of society's consciousness, greatness was something to deny, limit, or avoid. Life became mediocre.

There were a few free thinkers who dared to be great. They challenged the church and refused to listen to the rules. Today, we would refer to them as rebels. Jesus would have been considered a rebel because he challenged hypocrisy. Depending on the time and place, Jesus could have been called an outlaw or hippie.

So continue being a seeker, explorer and a teacher. Some people may see you as strange, rebellious, a trouble maker, or whatever other names they want to call you, but it doesn't matter what they think.

Thank you very much for your confidence and support.
You're welcome. Is there anything else you would like to know, Sheree?

Yes, I would like to know if learning to draw and paint is good for me.
Oh, yes darling. Drawing and painting is an expression of your inner self. As a human, you should have some form of self expression. By exploring art, you are allowing yourself access to the unlimited creative potential of yourself. You are allowing light, wonder and joy into your world and are giving your mind an opportunity to expand.

Art is a personal experience, therefore try not to judge or compare your art with others. Be an individual. There is no right or wrong in art. Just have fun.

That is easier said than done.
You are right. That's why many people dismiss their creative side by saying, "I have no talent." This is limited thinking, so don't buy into that idea. We must remain open and willing to experience different things. You are on the right track.

Thank you. I'll say good-bye now. We will write again soon.
Okay Darling. Good Night.

♥ ♥ ♥

For a long time my creativity has been in a slump. I remember loving to draw and color as a child for school projects. Lately I have again become interested in art. I think the excitement of the new house has renewed my long dormant desire to be creative. I also enjoy writing and have managed to maintain a diary since I was young. Writing has been my therapy over the years.

♥ ♥ ♥

January 2, 2001

Can you talk with me now, Poppa?
Hello Sheree, certainly I can.

Lately I have been battling two opposing sides of myself. One side of me is feeling pushed to plan my classes and start studying to complete my Ph.D., while the other side of me just wants to work at a slow pace and do some writing and a little reading.
So what are you asking me?

What side of myself do I honor?
You honor the side that makes you feel whole and healthy, as we discussed before.

What does that mean?
Well, stress in life can be motivating, but too much stress is not healthy. Pushing yourself into things can cause health problems. Right now it is good for you, and it brings you joy to read and write a little. This keeps you healthy and at peace.

Yes, but aren't I being lazy?
By whose definition are you calling yourself lazy?

By society's definition, it is important to be productive.
Tell me why it is not productive to sit here and write to me or to read your spiritual books?

I understand what you are saying, but if I am not making money or helping people I feel like I am not being productive in my life.
Oh I see you have a belief problem. Well, remember that what you believe, you create. So your belief is that reading and writing or drawing is not productive, but stressing and pushing yourself to do things you don't really want to do, is productive. When you write to me, it helps you feel better. Is this not true?

Yes, that's true.
Well, when you read it helps you understand life and yourself on a deeper level. As you learn to draw, you are teaching yourself to be observant and to look at things from different perspectives. So basically, you are telling me it's not productive to feel better, to understand life from a different viewpoint, and to see things from a new understanding.

Well, when you put it that way...
This is the only way you can look at it. You must not judge 'productivity' from other people's standards, only by your own, based on what you learn and create for your soul growth. Know that this is the right road for you, even if others may not find this road productive for them.

Thank you, should I put my teaching and study work on hold?
It's rather a question of timing. Is teaching and your study-work what you really want to do right now?

No, Poppa, it's not.
Then wait until you feel the calling.

Okay. Thank you for your help.
You are welcome, Darling.

♥ ♥ ♥

I have been a striver most of my life. In school, I worked hard to insure that I would receive certificates. Then I endeavored to win awards for dancing and swimming. When my efforts paid off and I won awards in these areas, my need to succeed then carried me to my college graduation.

Thereafter, in my work-life, especially in gaining knowledge for my spiritual growth, I often find myself reading four to five books at the same time, in addition to Journaling and recording my dreams for my dream study.

Some of this 'need to succeed' probably came out of my need for the approval of others or maybe my lack of love for myself.

In tonight's conversation with my grandfather, he pointed out to me that it was okay for me to stop and honor myself.

♥ ♥ ♥

39

February 5, 2001

It is 2001 and everything is changing for me, some good and some bad. I spoke with my girlfriend, Heidi, a few weeks ago and I can honestly say I am jealous. She has met a wonderful man who is open, loving and adores her. I, on the other hand, have not been happy in my marriage for such a long time. I keep feeling that if a special man exists for Heidi, it should exist for me, also.

It is hard to accept that my marriage has failed, but I can't deny my feelings any longer. Even my dreams at night are showing me this.

Lately, whenever I have some free time, I watch movies and the romantic ones always make me cry. Of course, in the movies everything usually works out for the best for the two lovers.

One day I found myself writing out my choices:
1. Stay emotionally unfulfilled in my marriage
2. Become his roommate
3. Risk a new life – divorce and start over

When I looked at my options, I realized our marriage is really over. I am too young to stay in a loveless marriage for the rest of my life or until he decides to move on. I would rather divorce now and be alone than remain in this marriage any longer. My heart could not be denied. I didn't know at this point what my future held, so I turned to my grandfather for comfort.

♥ ♥ ♥

Hi Poppa.
Hello, I am sorry you are so sad.

I am sad and it hurts so much.
I know Darling and I wish I could hold you in my arms and tell you everything will be okay.

Why was I so stupid and why did I stay so long?
You are not stupid. That is not the word to use.

But if I wasn't stupid, why did I stay so long in this marriage.
You know why you stayed–to have your children, to do your work, and to love Scott.

Yes, but he doesn't love me.
That is not the way it is. He loves you the best he can.

But he could make it better if he really tried.
No, not without help.

He doesn't want to seek help.
That is what you have to face. He doesn't want help. He, therefore, doesn't want to get well.

If he loved me enough, he would want to get help.
Yes, I agree.

That hurts.
I know Sheree.

What am I supposed to do now?
You have to go forward with your life.

Why? What is the point?
The point is you are a lovely girl with two beautiful children. You have a new home, wonderful friends, your work and that's more than some people could ever hope for. You have a lot going for you.

But the pain is so awful. This sadness hangs over me like a heavy black thunder cloud casting doubt on everything I do and think.
You must have faith that a better life awaits you, that a loving, affectionate man awaits you.

From where I am sitting, that seems very unlikely.
Well, from where I am sitting, Sheree, it seems very likely. You have so much work to do. You need to focus on your mission and be open to whom you will meet in the process.

I am so tired.
Tired! I don't want to hear it. You have books to write, people to teach, children to raise and love to share.

What do I do about Scott?
He has made his decision that he can't or doesn't want a future with you. He has made himself very clear on that point, so you must accept it and move forward.

How am I going to manage financially?
That is not going to be a problem for you.

How can you say that? We have no savings and Scott has no permanent job. How am I going to support the kids and myself?
The money will be there.

127

How, Poppa?
I have been shown that sufficient funds are coming to you. I don't know the details, but I can see you managing well financially with the children.

But our monthly bills are several thousand dollars.
That will not be a problem.

Can you be specific about the time frame?
Soon, very soon, is as specific as I can be.

Can you tell me if there will be another man for me?
Yes, I am very certain.

When will he come?
That has already been decided.

What do you mean?
The man is ready now.

Really?
The way to accept this is to release the past, face the present, and live in the NOW. It's over with Scott.

Okay, I accept it. Now what?
You must become at peace with yourself and all else will take care of itself.

♥ ♥ ♥

September, 2003

Poppa promised that a special man would come into my life. In February, 2002, I met Sam. We experienced an instant recognition. I believe he is the man I talked to in my head at the beach.

We have many parallels in our lives. Sam was married the same year as I was, a month apart in 1986. We were both divorced within two weeks of each other. He never had children but always wanted them. He is wonderful to my two boys. Poppa was right when he said I would never be cold again. I feel very loved and supported by Sam. Not long after he came into my life, he gave me the money to open the Shiloh Spiritual Center, and now he works by my side.

♥ ♥ ♥

February 25, 2001

Hi Poppa.
Hello, Sheree. Mazel Tov. You did it. You let Scott go.

Why do you say Mazel Tov?
I say Mazel Tov because you completed your contract. You did it.

What contract are you speaking of?
You promised to come here and love Scott and have children by him and you did that. So we say Mazel Tov, Sheree because you honored your truth. You honored what you felt inside.

♥ ♥ ♥

Mazel Tov is a Jewish greeting, which means congratulations or good luck.

♥ ♥ ♥

41

March 5, 2001

Hi Pops.
Hi Darling, I am so glad to see you feeling a lot better.

I am feeling so much better. Thank you for the inspiration and guidance you have given me.
It will be wonderful, Sheree, this new life that is going to open for you. Things are moving fast.

I have something important to talk to you about. Scott wants to settle out of court using a mediator.
I am aware of that.

Is this something I should agree with?
Yes, you should agree to the mediator because it's not necessary to delay this divorce. You need to get on with your life.

I am still worried about having enough money to live.
Don't worry, you will have clients and the money will be there to take care of all your needs.

Oh, I hope so Poppa.

♥ ♥ ♥

Money is a big concern for me and trust is something I need to adopt. For the past sixteen years, Scott's money paid the living expenses and the money from my clients allowed us to travel. For years, he told me that if we divorced, I would be penniless and living on the streets. I no longer believed him, but I was still nervous about it.

Fortunately, I did not give in to my fear and held firm to the belief that everything would be okay. At times during this process I was angry with myself for staying in my marriage so long, especially when I knew, even early on in the marriage, that I was unhappy.

I waited until I was twenty-seven before I married. I really believed that Scott was my soul-mate. My parents divorced when I was eight and I always told myself I would never divorce regardless of the circumstances. I promised myself to always be faithful to my husband. I was, but there were times I was tempted. Our marriage is now over and I know I am making the correct decision for me and my children.

♥ ♥ ♥

42

March 9, 2001

Two weeks ago, I woke up in the morning to the song, "Bye, Bye, Miss American Pie," playing in my head. Scott was gone, and so, in a way was my illusion of marriage as I wanted it to be, versus the truth of what my life was really like. Well, I did it. I faced my feelings. On some days I felt free and on others I actually felt joyful. I will not say it was easy because often I would panic. There were times in the last few weeks where I felt completely helpless, but I got through them and now I turn to my Poppa for encouragement.

♥ ♥ ♥

Hi Pops.
Hello Darling. Well, you did it.

Yes, thank you, I feel lucky that I was brave enough to do it.
Yes, that is true, Sheree, millions of people don't and they remain prisoners of their fears.

Well, I am glad I am free and I now feel wonderful.
Your whole energy has changed. Your smile and your laughter is real, so go out and enjoy.

I plan to do just that.
   Be careful though, don't be deceived. Be true to your inner voice and don't dismiss warning signs.

I will try not to, Poppa. I am still a little concerned about money, though.
   As I have told you before, everything will work out well financially for you.

Are you sure?
   Yes, you will not lose your home and you and the children will manage wonderfully.

Thank you for your support.
   You are welcome. Remember, you are never alone.

I know, but sometimes it can feel like I am.
   Of course it can, but that is usually in times that you are disconnected from spirit. As soon as you meditate and open your heart, love pours in from God and all the angels around you, especially your guardian angel.

I am starting to get okay with uncertainty. Deepak Chopra says on the *Seven Spiritual Laws* tape, "…in uncertainty, all possible solutions can come about." Well, I am certainly there. Yet, I know I will be okay.
   That is wonderful, Darling. Keep up the good spirits.
   Love, Poppa.

43

March 13, 2001

Hi Poppa.
Hi Darling.

I am starting to feel life directed again.
That is wonderful! We have all been doing a lot of work to show you who you are. You must not forget all the help you have in the spirit world.

Thank you, that is encouraging to hear.
You are moving along nicely and soon life is going to be filled with one exciting adventure after another. You will have no time to be sad. The realizations you've come to are the right path. Therefore, it's time for you to be out there in the public eye. The children will be fine and you will have a lot of support and help. Your work is now truly beginning.

What can I expect?
Many surprises and a lot of wonderful synchronicity events are in store for you. The time is now for the world to know who you are.

What about all of our conversations? Should I put them all into a book?
Yes, Sheree, you know we had arranged this with each other. I would be honored for you to do that.

Should I find a publisher or self-publish?
Your friend was right last night, it's better for you to self-publish that way you will have the book right away to promote.

Are we going to continue to write together?
We can go on writing until you are old if you want to, but I feel that you have enough material to make a wonderful book.

Are you saying we are done?
I am saying we will never be done; I will always be here for you because death is never the end. Death is kind of like a divorce. Always remember, that when one door closes, another door always opens. I am here if you ever need me, I will answer any questions you may have.

Are you sure there is nothing else you want to share with me for this book?
I do want to share that when you are walking in faith, miracles come into your life.

Do you have an idea for a title for the book we are writing together?
That will be up to you. It is not necessary to put my picture on the cover. You can put it on the inside if you want to.

What should I put on the cover?
That also will be up to you and I know the right idea will come to you.

What is my next step?
Your next step is to get your work organized, typed and formatted. Then you can work with a self-publishing company. Mazel Tov.

Thank you for being my grandfather.
Stay strong and positive Sheree. Many blessings are coming your way.

I love you.
I love you too.

Bye Poppa.

The End

Directions for Contacting Your Loved One on the Other Side

We all have the ability to communicate with our loved ones, but we need patience, faith, an open heart and mind.

You will need writing material.

A quiet place to sit without being disturbed.

Do not have preconceptions about what will happen or in what form the information may come to you.

You may write in forms which you have not used before.

You may experience a charge of electric energy going through your arm and hand. This happens often when the thoughts come fast.

Take a deep breath and relax and ask for God's protection.

At first it may seem that all you are doing is scribbling on the page.

Take your time and allow the thoughts to come.

If you are directing your questions to a person on the other side, ask that person a question, or look at a picture of the person as you ask a question.

Trust your thoughts and write them down.